降去神通

AVATAR

THE LAST AIRBENDER™

Created by
Bryan Konietzko
Michael Dante DiMartino

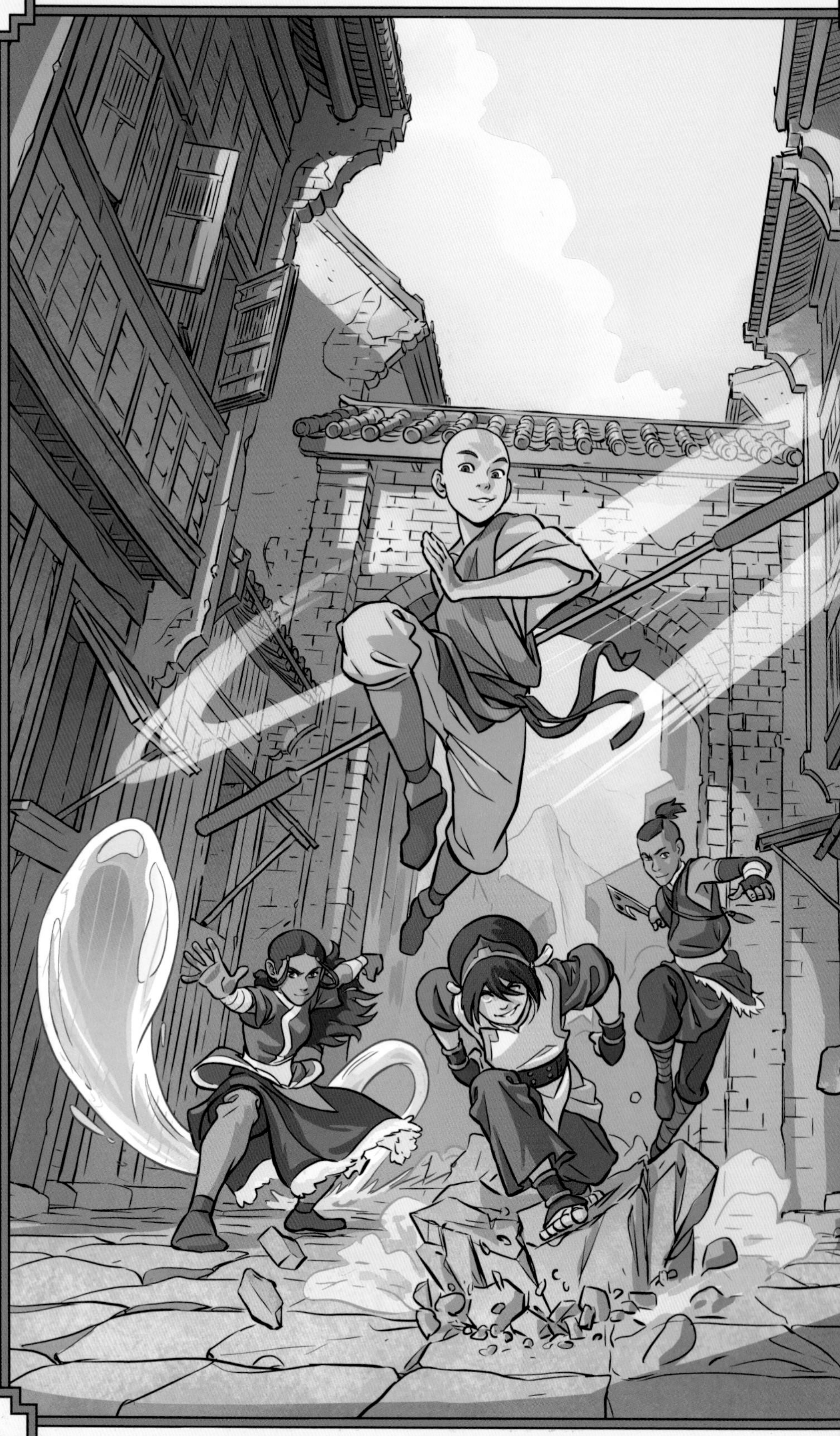

nickelodeon TM

降击神通

AVATAR

THE LAST AIRBENDER TM

IMBALANCE · PART ONE

script
FAITH ERIN HICKS

art
PETER WARTMAN

colors
RYAN HILL

lettering
**RICHARD STARKINGS &
COMICRAFT'S JIMMY BETANCOURT**

DARK HORSE BOOKS

president and publisher
MIKE RICHARDSON

editor
DAVE MARSHALL

associate editor
RACHEL ROBERTS

collection designer
SARAH TERRY

digital art technician
CHRISTIANNE GOUDREAU

martial arts consultant and model
TODD BALTHAZOR

Special thanks to Linda Lee, James Salerno, and Joan Hilty
at Nickelodeon, and to Bryan Konietzko and Michael Dante DiMartino.

Published by **Dark Horse Books**
A division of Dark Horse Comics, Inc.
10956 SE Main Street, Milwaukie, OR 97222

DarkHorse.com
Nick.com

To find a comics shop in your area, visit comicshoplocator.com

First edition: October 2018 | ISBN 978-1-50670-489-0

1 3 5 7 9 10 8 6 4 2
Printed in China

Neil Hankerson Executive Vice President • Tom Weddle Chief Financial Officer • Randy Stradley Vice President of Publishing • Nick McWhorter Chief Business Development Officer • Matt Parkinson Vice President of Marketing • Dale LaFountain Vice President of Information Technology • Cara Niece Vice President of Production and Scheduling • Mark Bernardi Vice President of Book Trade and Digital Sales • Ken Lizzi General Counsel • Dave Marshall Editor in Chief • Davey Estrada Editorial Director • Chris Warner Senior Books Editor • Cary Grazzini Director of Specialty Projects • Lia Ribacchi Art Director • Vanessa Todd-Holmes Director of Print Purchasing • Matt Dryer Director of Digital Art and Prepress • Michael Gombos Director of International Publishing and Licensing • Kari Yadro Director of Custom Programs

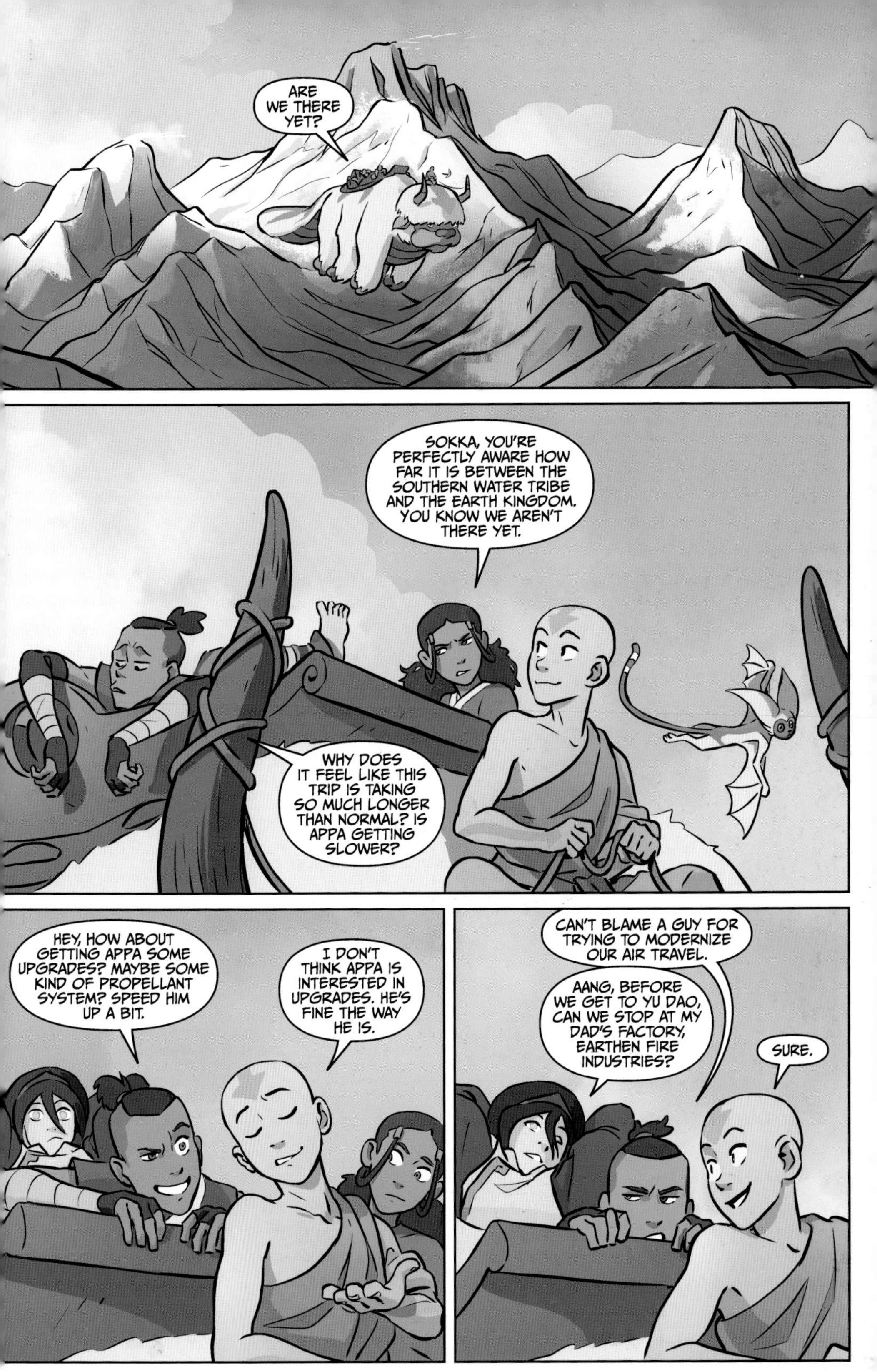
ARE WE THERE YET?
SOKKA, YOU'RE PERFECTLY AWARE HOW FAR IT IS BETWEEN THE SOUTHERN WATER TRIBE AND THE EARTH KINGDOM. YOU KNOW WE AREN'T THERE YET.
WHY DOES IT FEEL LIKE THIS TRIP IS TAKING SO MUCH LONGER THAN NORMAL? IS APPA GETTING SLOWER?
HEY, HOW ABOUT GETTING APPA SOME UPGRADES? MAYBE SOME KIND OF PROPELLANT SYSTEM? SPEED HIM UP A BIT.
I DON'T THINK APPA IS INTERESTED IN UPGRADES. HE'S FINE THE WAY HE IS.
CAN'T BLAME A GUY FOR TRYING TO MODERNIZE OUR AIR TRAVEL.
AANG, BEFORE WE GET TO YU DAO, CAN WE STOP AT MY DAD'S FACTORY, EARTHEN FIRE INDUSTRIES?
SURE.

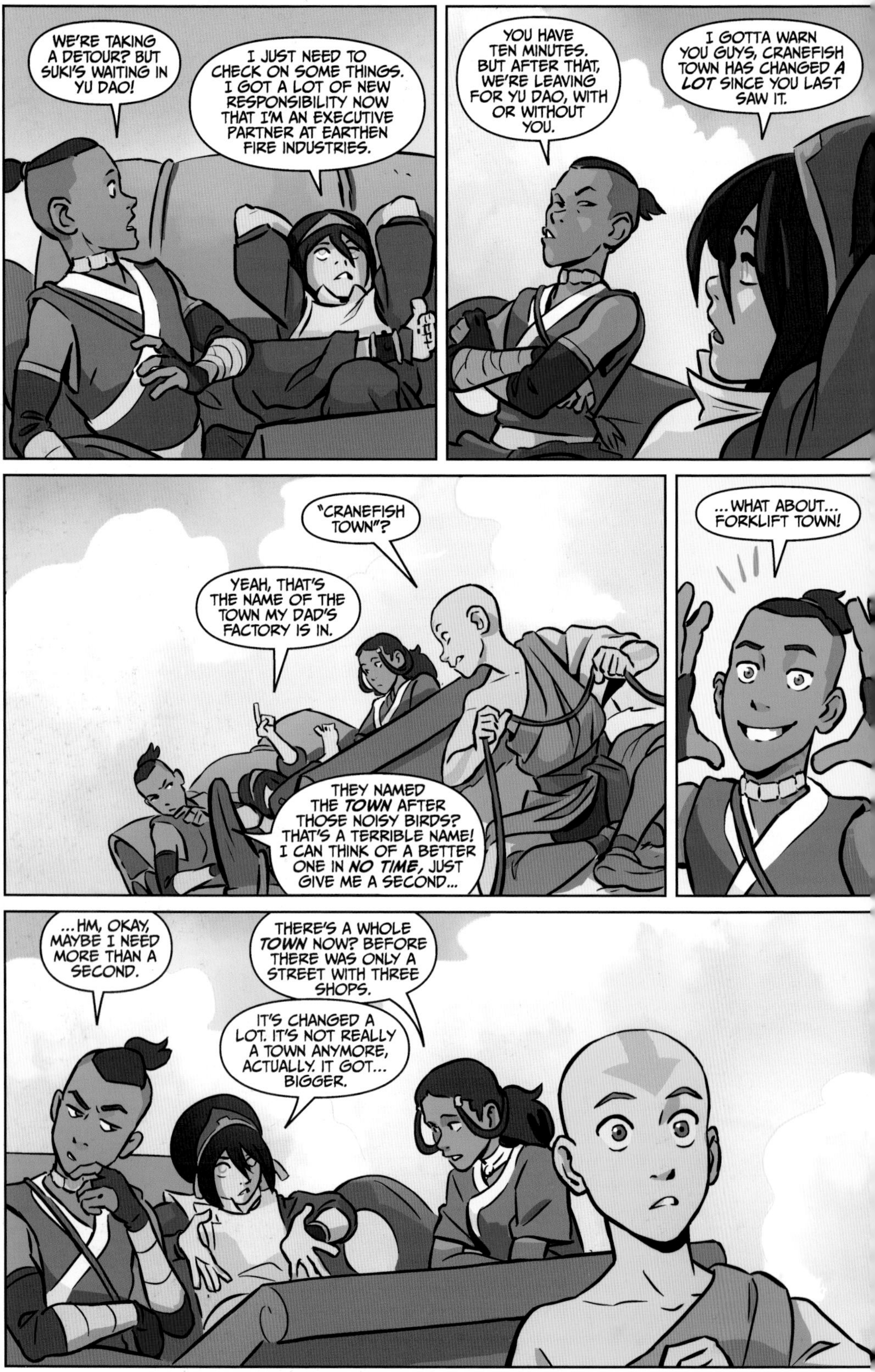
WE'RE TAKING A DETOUR? BUT SUKI'S WAITING IN YU DAO!
I JUST NEED TO CHECK ON SOME THINGS. I GOT A LOT OF NEW RESPONSIBILITY NOW THAT I'M AN EXECUTIVE PARTNER AT EARTHEN FIRE INDUSTRIES.
YOU HAVE TEN MINUTES. BUT AFTER THAT, WE'RE LEAVING FOR YU DAO, WITH OR WITHOUT YOU.
I GOTTA WARN YOU GUYS, CRANEFISH TOWN HAS CHANGED A LOT SINCE YOU LAST SAW IT.
"CRANEFISH TOWN"?
YEAH, THAT'S THE NAME OF THE TOWN MY DAD'S FACTORY IS IN.
THEY NAMED THE TOWN AFTER THOSE NOISY BIRDS? THAT'S A TERRIBLE NAME! I CAN THINK OF A BETTER ONE IN NO TIME, JUST GIVE ME A SECOND...
...WHAT ABOUT... FORKLIFT TOWN!
...HM, OKAY, MAYBE I NEED MORE THAN A SECOND.
THERE'S A WHOLE TOWN NOW? BEFORE THERE WAS ONLY A STREET WITH THREE SHOPS.
IT'S CHANGED A LOT. IT'S NOT REALLY A TOWN ANYMORE, ACTUALLY. IT GOT... BIGGER.

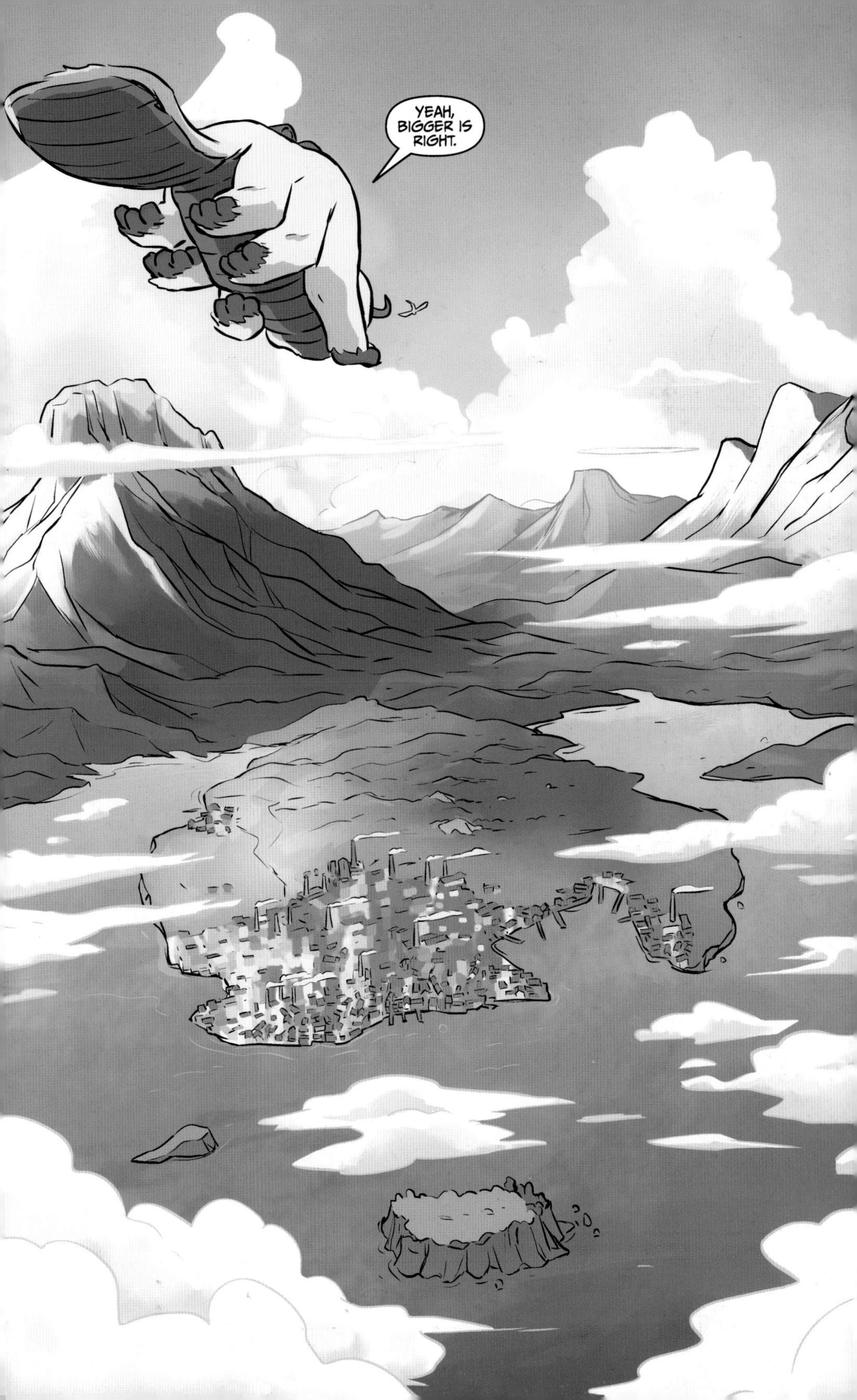
YEAH, BIGGER IS RIGHT.

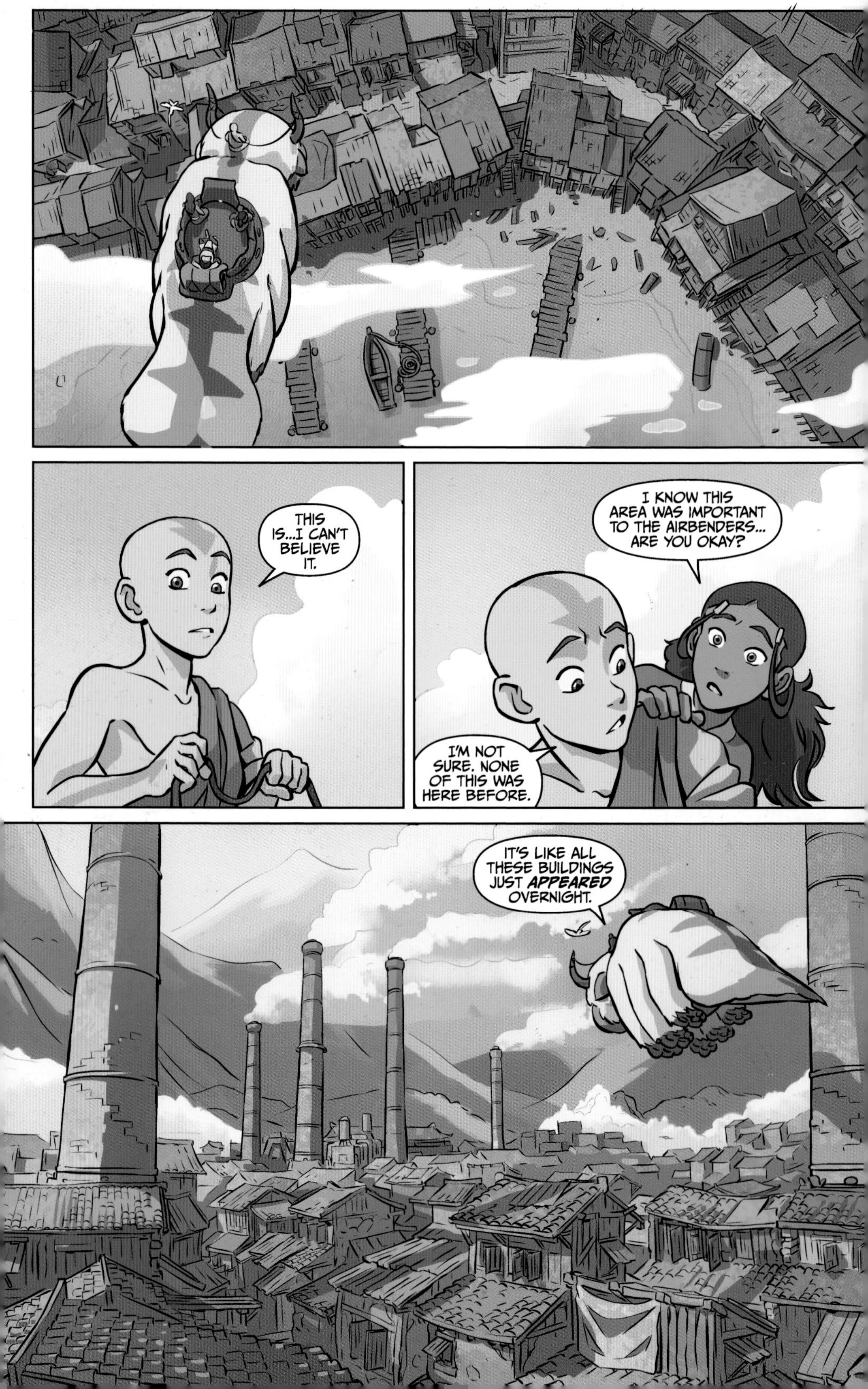
THIS IS...I CAN'T BELIEVE IT.
I KNOW THIS AREA WAS IMPORTANT TO THE AIRBENDERS... ARE YOU OKAY?
I'M NOT SURE. NONE OF THIS WAS HERE BEFORE.
IT'S LIKE ALL THESE BUILDINGS JUST *APPEARED* OVERNIGHT.

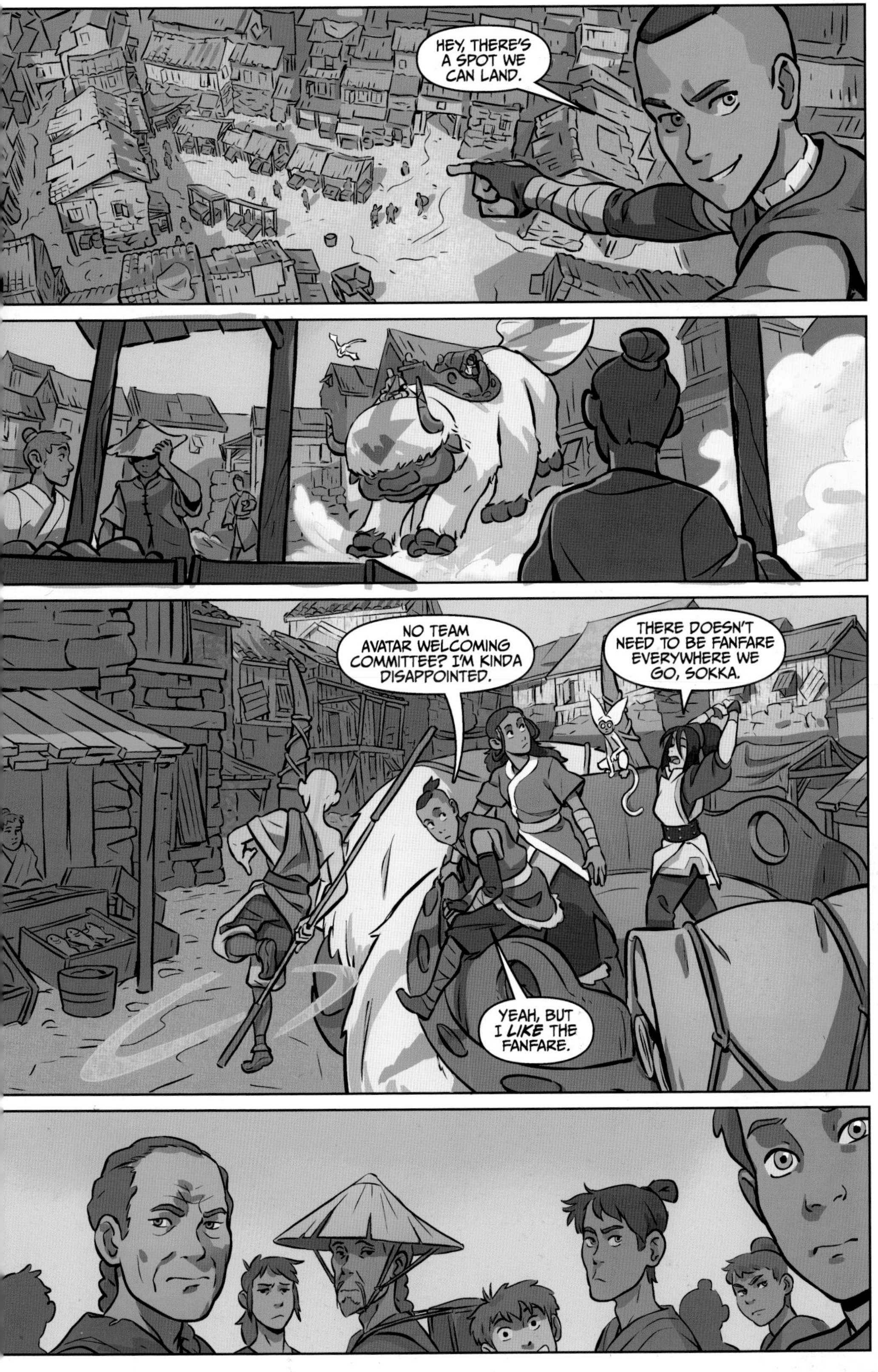
HEY, THERE'S A SPOT WE CAN LAND.
NO TEAM AVATAR WELCOMING COMMITTEE? I'M KINDA DISAPPOINTED.
THERE DOESN'T NEED TO BE FANFARE EVERYWHERE WE GO, SOKKA.
YEAH, BUT I *LIKE* THE FANFARE.

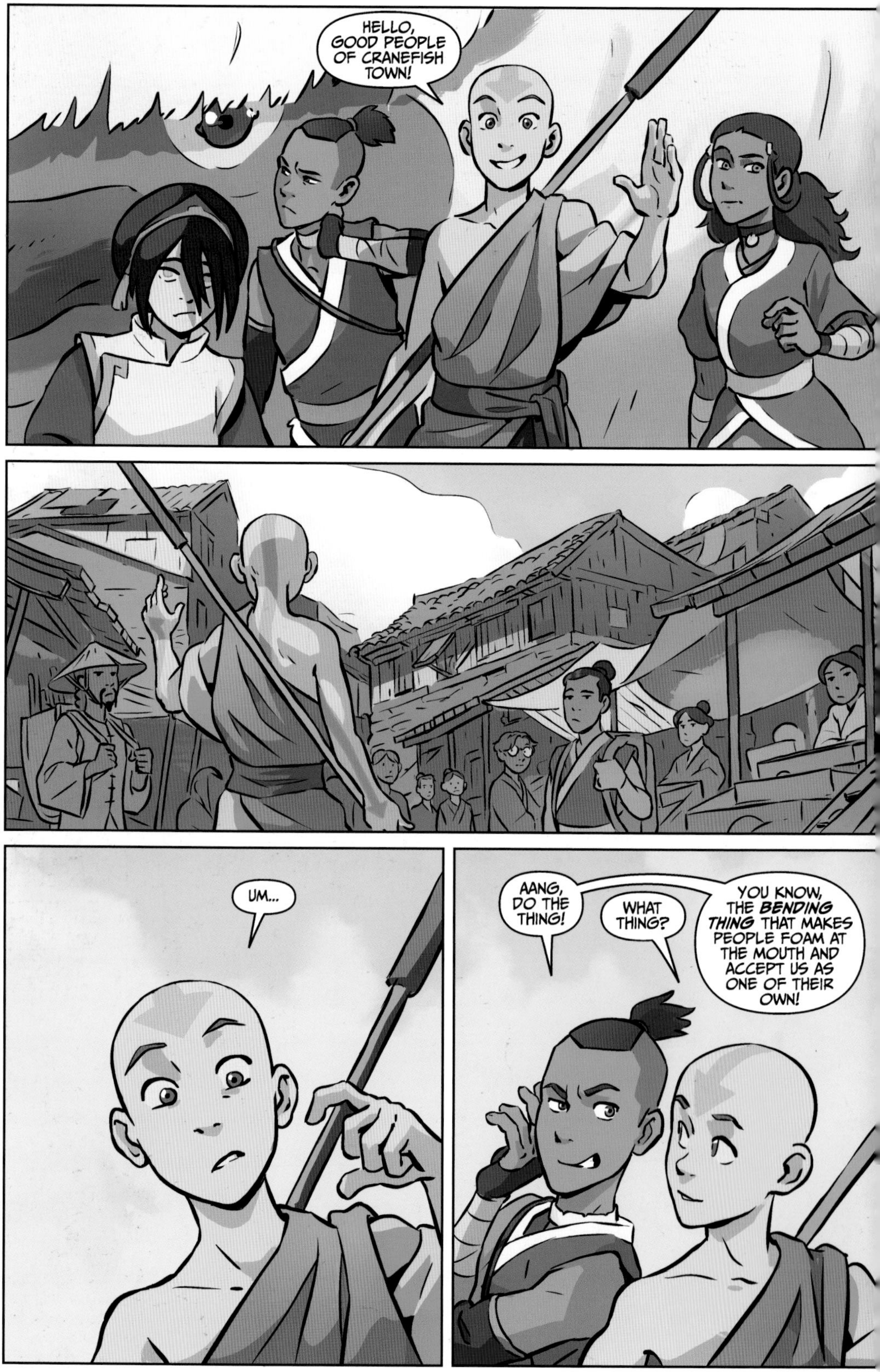
HELLO, GOOD PEOPLE OF CRANEFISH TOWN!
UM...
AANG, DO THE THING!
WHAT THING?
YOU KNOW, THE **BENDING THING** THAT MAKES PEOPLE FOAM AT THE MOUTH AND ACCEPT US AS ONE OF THEIR OWN!

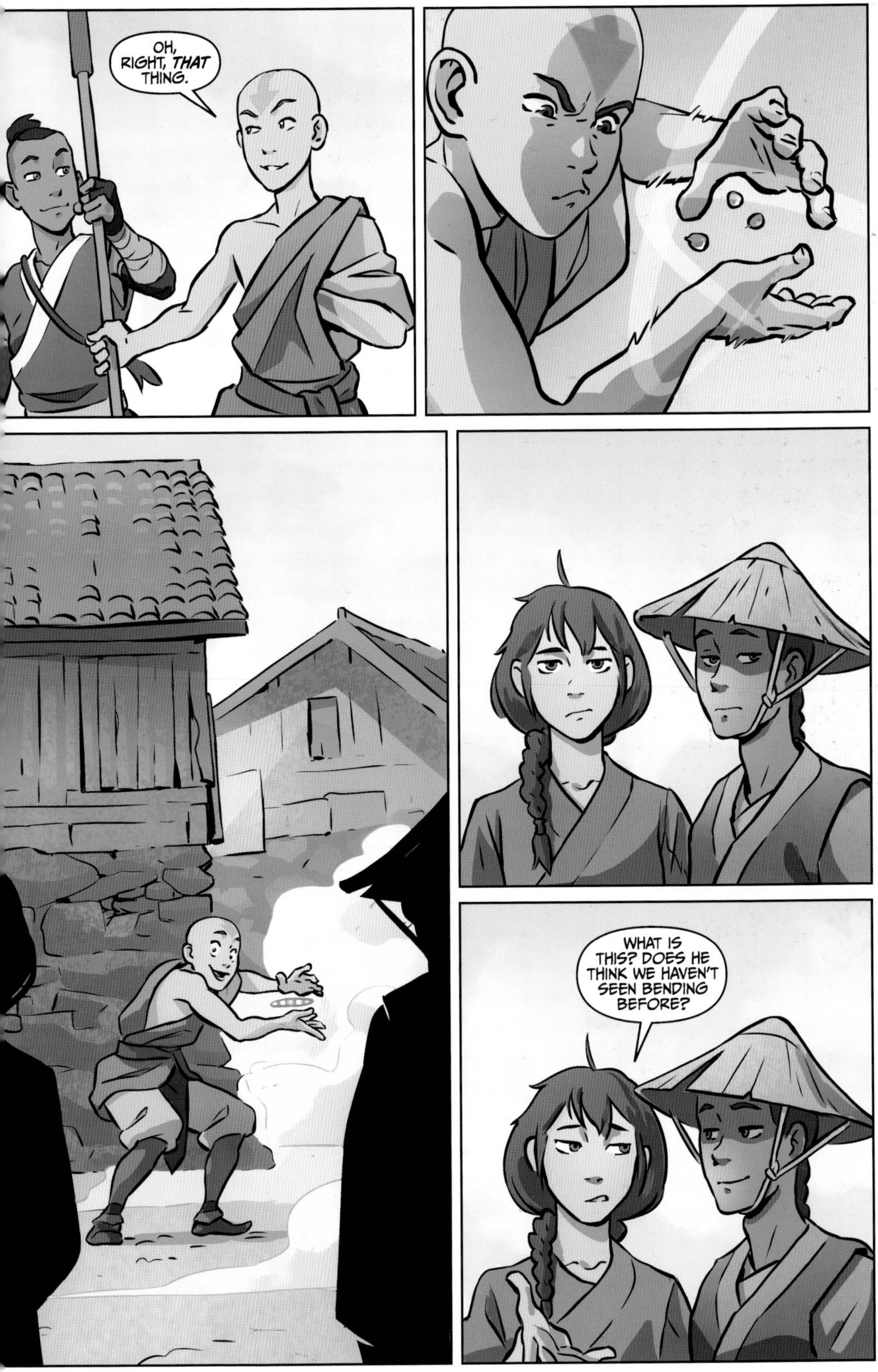
OH, RIGHT, *THAT* THING.
WHAT IS THIS? DOES HE THINK WE HAVEN'T SEEN BENDING BEFORE?

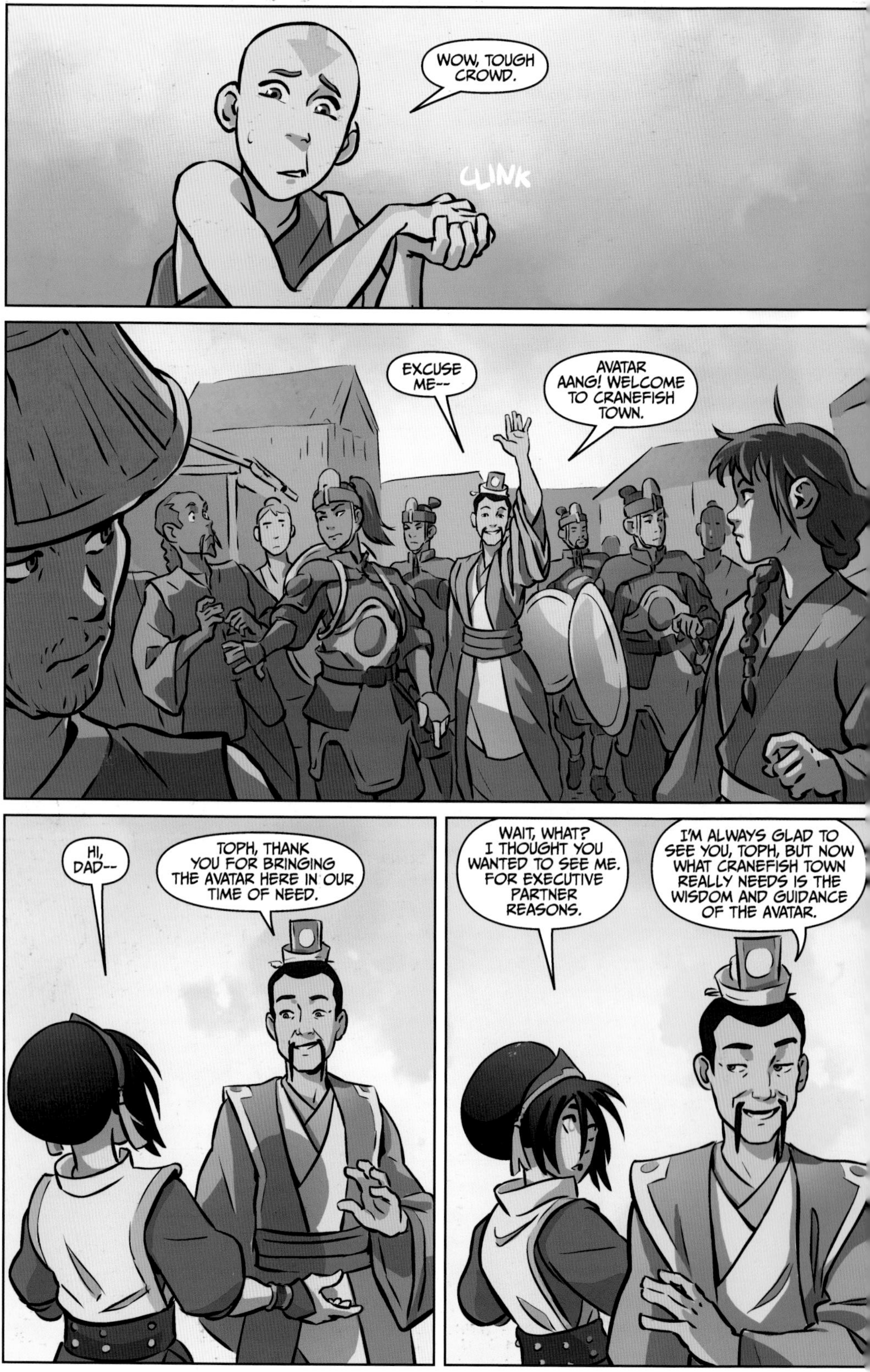
WOW, TOUGH CROWD.
CLINK
EXCUSE ME--
AVATAR AANG! WELCOME TO CRANEFISH TOWN.
HI, DAD--
TOPH, THANK YOU FOR BRINGING THE AVATAR HERE IN OUR TIME OF NEED.
WAIT, WHAT? I THOUGHT YOU WANTED TO SEE ME. FOR EXECUTIVE PARTNER REASONS.
I'M ALWAYS GLAD TO SEE YOU, TOPH, BUT NOW WHAT CRANEFISH TOWN REALLY NEEDS IS THE WISDOM AND GUIDANCE OF THE AVATAR.

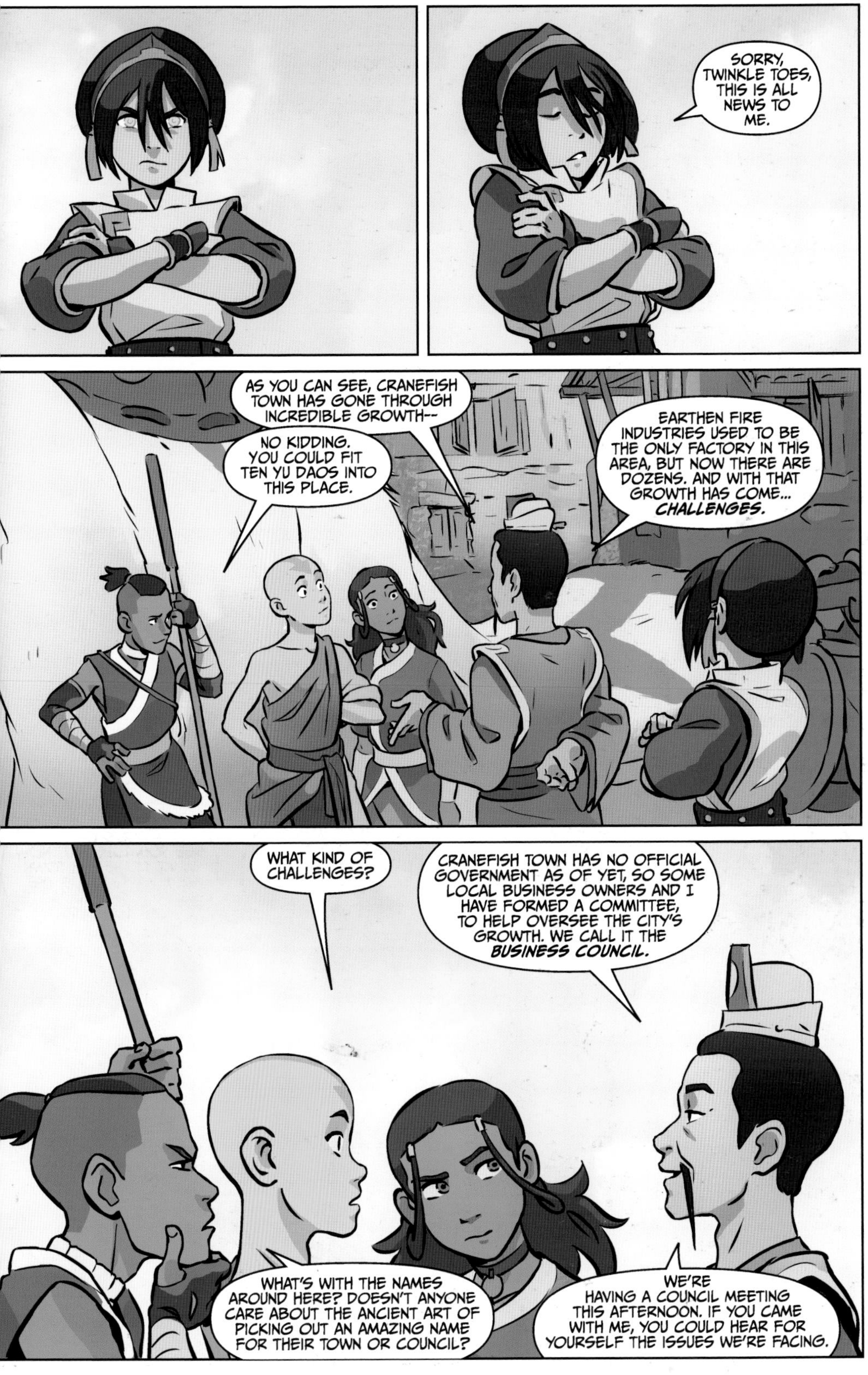
SORRY, TWINKLE TOES, THIS IS ALL NEWS TO ME.
AS YOU CAN SEE, CRANEFISH TOWN HAS GONE THROUGH INCREDIBLE GROWTH--
NO KIDDING. YOU COULD FIT TEN YU DAOS INTO THIS PLACE.
EARTHEN FIRE INDUSTRIES USED TO BE THE ONLY FACTORY IN THIS AREA, BUT NOW THERE ARE DOZENS. AND WITH THAT GROWTH HAS COME... CHALLENGES.
WHAT KIND OF CHALLENGES?
CRANEFISH TOWN HAS NO OFFICIAL GOVERNMENT AS OF YET, SO SOME LOCAL BUSINESS OWNERS AND I HAVE FORMED A COMMITTEE, TO HELP OVERSEE THE CITY'S GROWTH. WE CALL IT THE BUSINESS COUNCIL.
WHAT'S WITH THE NAMES AROUND HERE? DOESN'T ANYONE CARE ABOUT THE ANCIENT ART OF PICKING OUT AN AMAZING NAME FOR THEIR TOWN OR COUNCIL?
WE'RE HAVING A COUNCIL MEETING THIS AFTERNOON. IF YOU CAME WITH ME, YOU COULD HEAR FOR YOURSELF THE ISSUES WE'RE FACING.

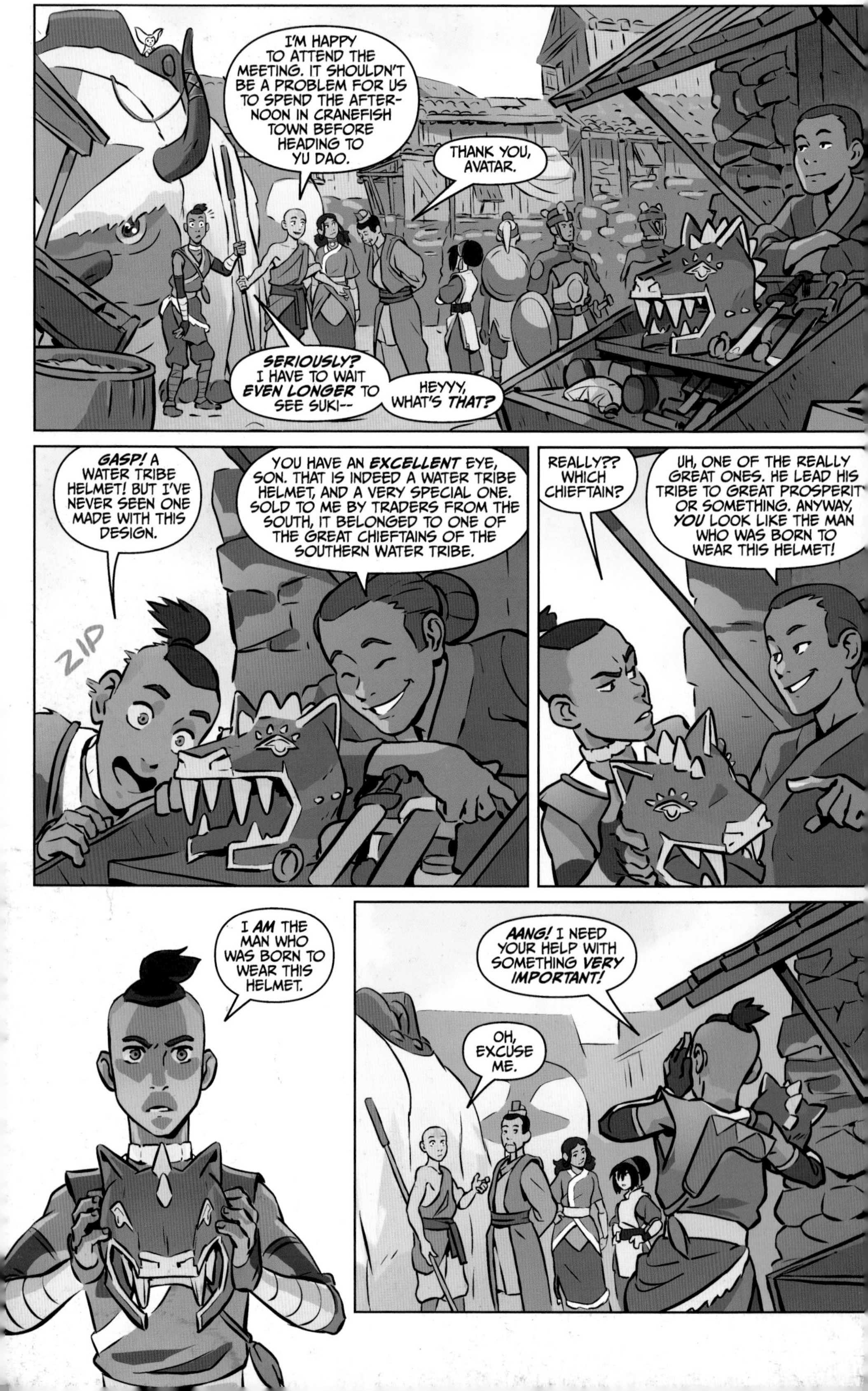
I'M HAPPY TO ATTEND THE MEETING. IT SHOULDN'T BE A PROBLEM FOR US TO SPEND THE AFTERNOON IN CRANEFISH TOWN BEFORE HEADING TO YU DAO.
THANK YOU, AVATAR.
SERIOUSLY? I HAVE TO WAIT EVEN LONGER TO SEE SUKI--
HEYYY, WHAT'S THAT?
GASP! A WATER TRIBE HELMET! BUT I'VE NEVER SEEN ONE MADE WITH THIS DESIGN.
ZIP
YOU HAVE AN EXCELLENT EYE, SON. THAT IS INDEED A WATER TRIBE HELMET, AND A VERY SPECIAL ONE. SOLD TO ME BY TRADERS FROM THE SOUTH, IT BELONGED TO ONE OF THE GREAT CHIEFTAINS OF THE SOUTHERN WATER TRIBE.
REALLY?? WHICH CHIEFTAIN?
UH, ONE OF THE REALLY GREAT ONES. HE LEAD HIS TRIBE TO GREAT PROSPERIT OR SOMETHING. ANYWAY, YOU LOOK LIKE THE MAN WHO WAS BORN TO WEAR THIS HELMET!
I AM THE MAN WHO WAS BORN TO WEAR THIS HELMET.
AANG! I NEED YOUR HELP WITH SOMETHING VERY IMPORTANT!
OH, EXCUSE ME.

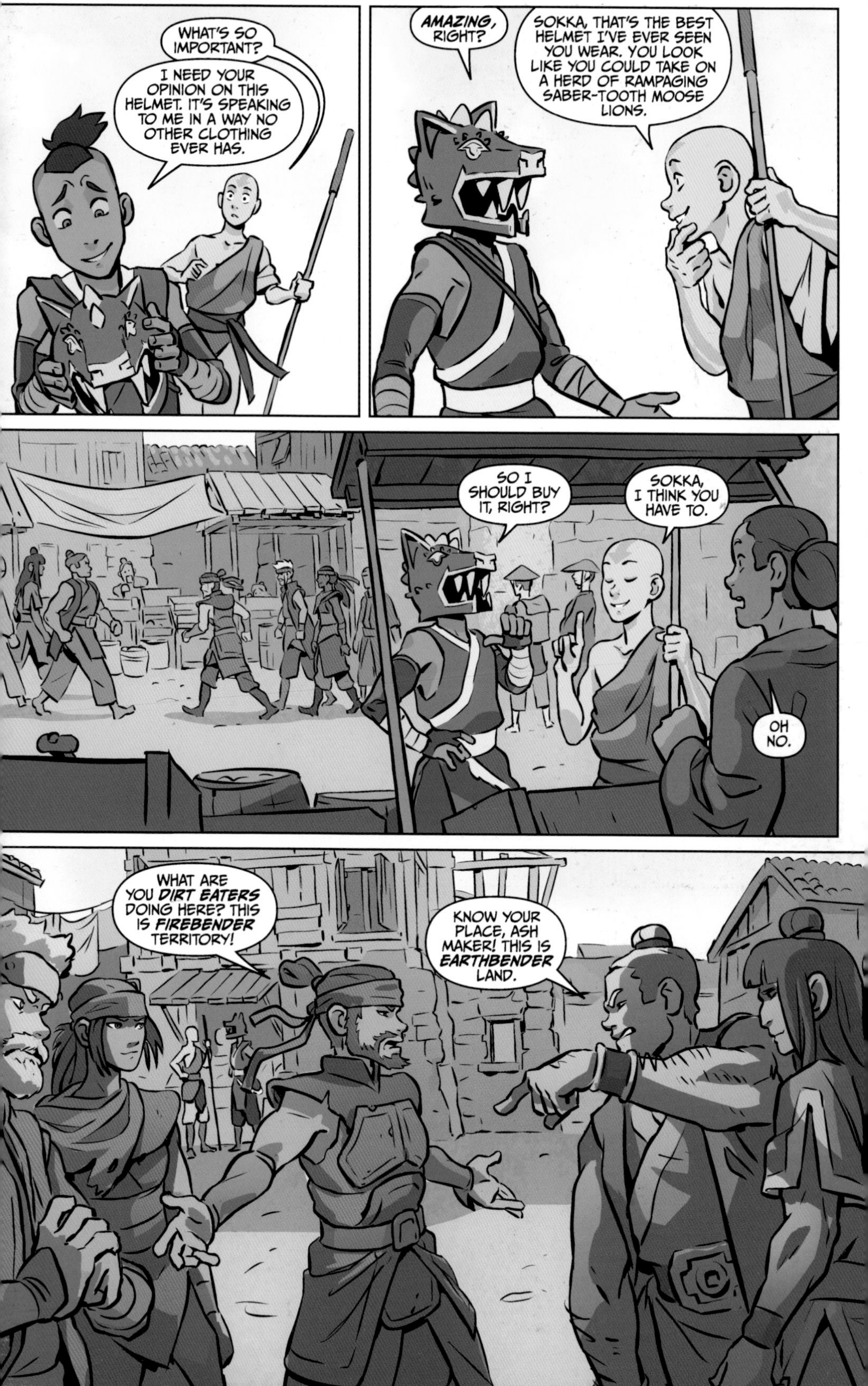
WHAT'S SO IMPORTANT?
I NEED YOUR OPINION ON THIS HELMET. IT'S SPEAKING TO ME IN A WAY NO OTHER CLOTHING EVER HAS.
AMAZING, RIGHT?
SOKKA, THAT'S THE BEST HELMET I'VE EVER SEEN YOU WEAR. YOU LOOK LIKE YOU COULD TAKE ON A HERD OF RAMPAGING SABER-TOOTH MOOSE LIONS.
SO I SHOULD BUY IT, RIGHT?
SOKKA, I THINK YOU HAVE TO.
OH NO.
WHAT ARE YOU *DIRT EATERS* DOING HERE? THIS IS *FIREBENDER* TERRITORY!
KNOW YOUR PLACE, ASH MAKER! THIS IS *EARTHBENDER* LAND.

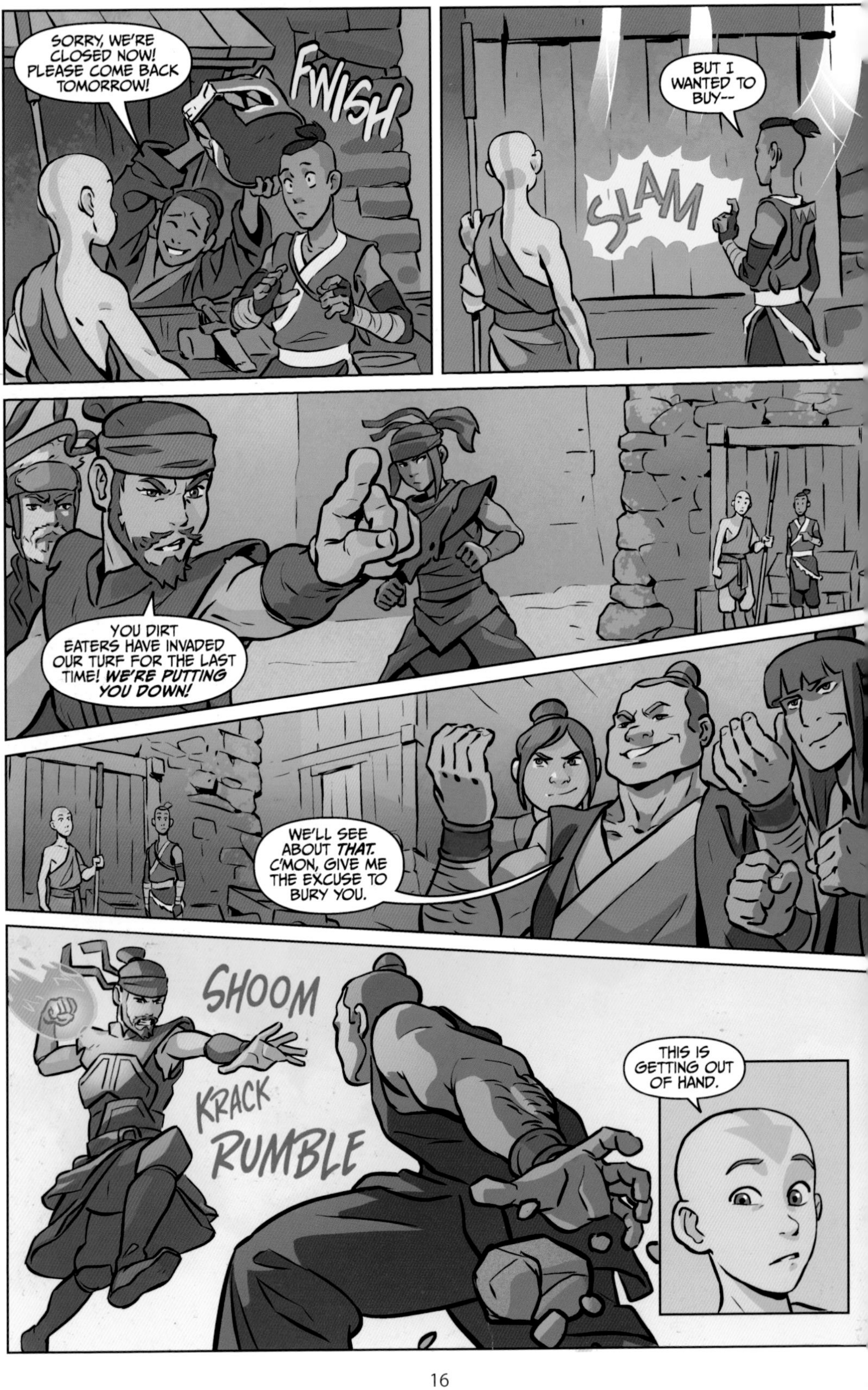
SORRY, WE'RE CLOSED NOW! PLEASE COME BACK TOMORROW!
FWISH
BUT I WANTED TO BUY--
SLAM
YOU DIRT EATERS HAVE INVADED OUR TURF FOR THE LAST TIME! WE'RE PUTTING YOU DOWN!
WE'LL SEE ABOUT THAT. C'MON, GIVE ME THE EXCUSE TO BURY YOU.
SHOOM
KRACK
RUMBLE
THIS IS GETTING OUT OF HAND.

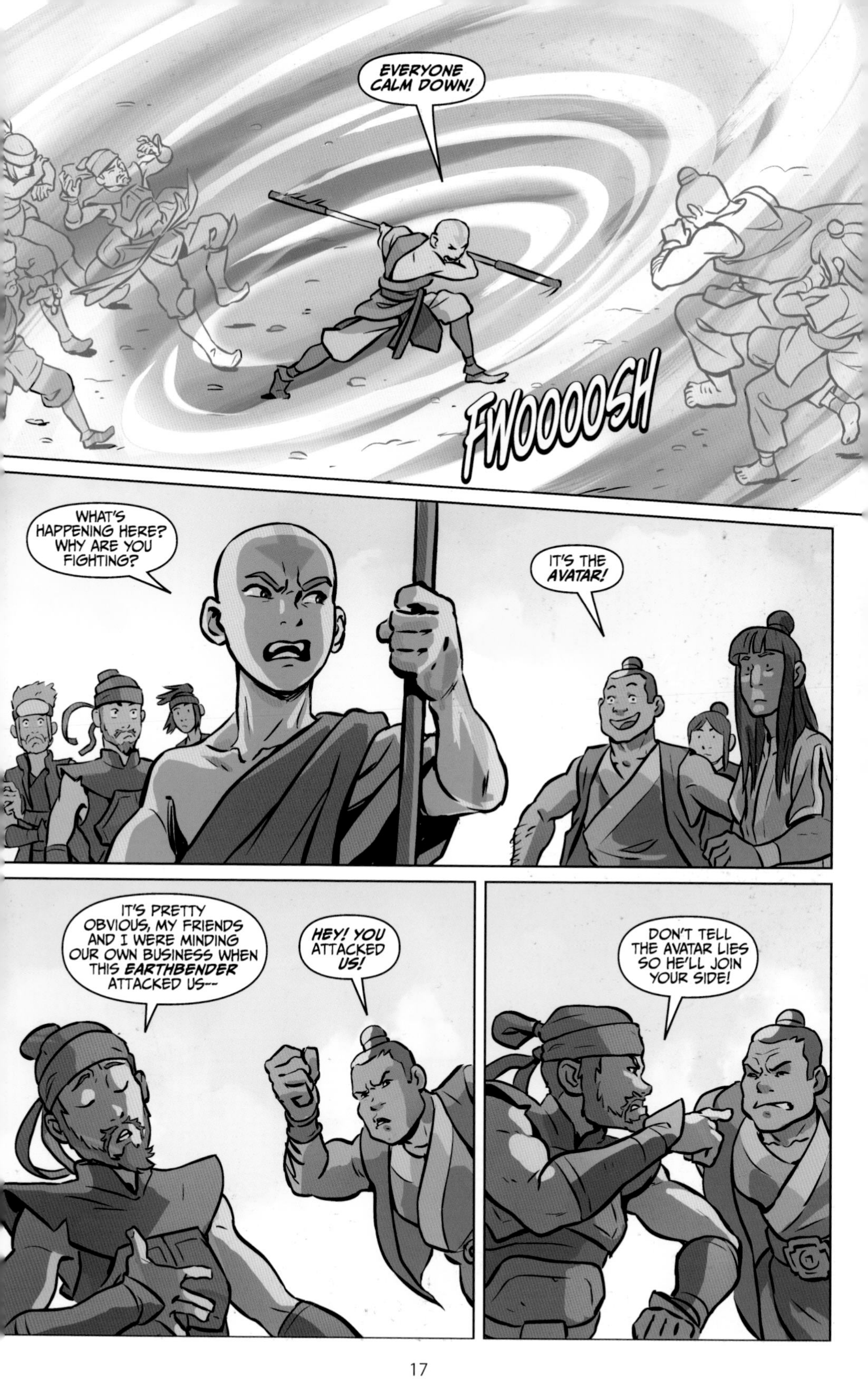
EVERYONE CALM DOWN!
FWOOOOSH
WHAT'S HAPPENING HERE? WHY ARE YOU FIGHTING?
IT'S THE AVATAR!
IT'S PRETTY OBVIOUS, MY FRIENDS AND I WERE MINDING OUR OWN BUSINESS WHEN THIS EARTHBENDER ATTACKED US--
HEY! YOU ATTACKED US!
DON'T TELL THE AVATAR LIES SO HE'LL JOIN YOUR SIDE!

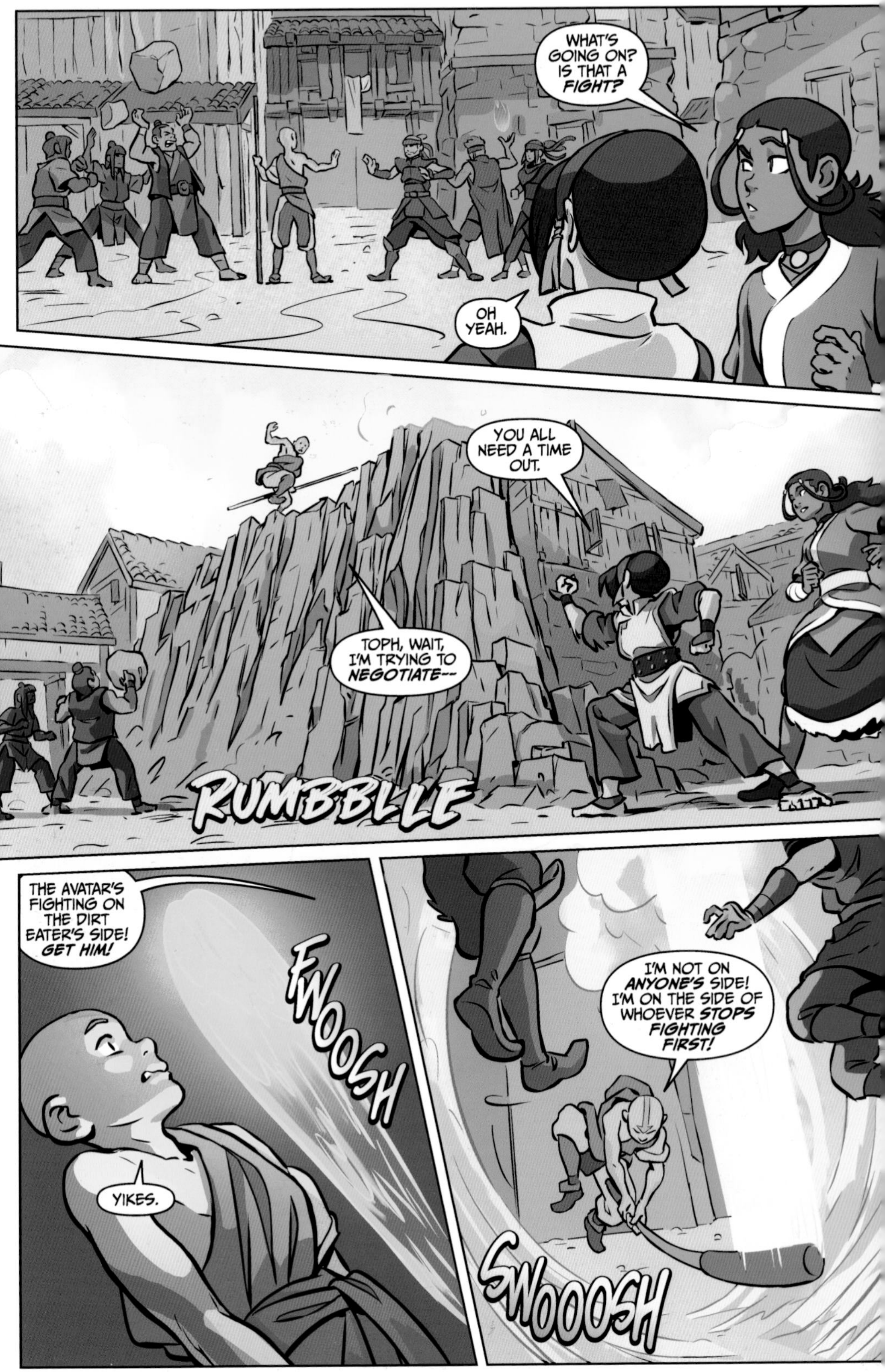
WHAT'S GOING ON? IS THAT A FIGHT?
OH YEAH.
YOU ALL NEED A TIME OUT.
TOPH, WAIT, I'M TRYING TO NEGOTIATE--
RUMBBLLE
THE AVATAR'S FIGHTING ON THE DIRT EATER'S SIDE! GET HIM!
FWOOSH
YIKES.
I'M NOT ON ANYONE'S SIDE! I'M ON THE SIDE OF WHOEVER STOPS FIGHTING FIRST!
SWOOOSH

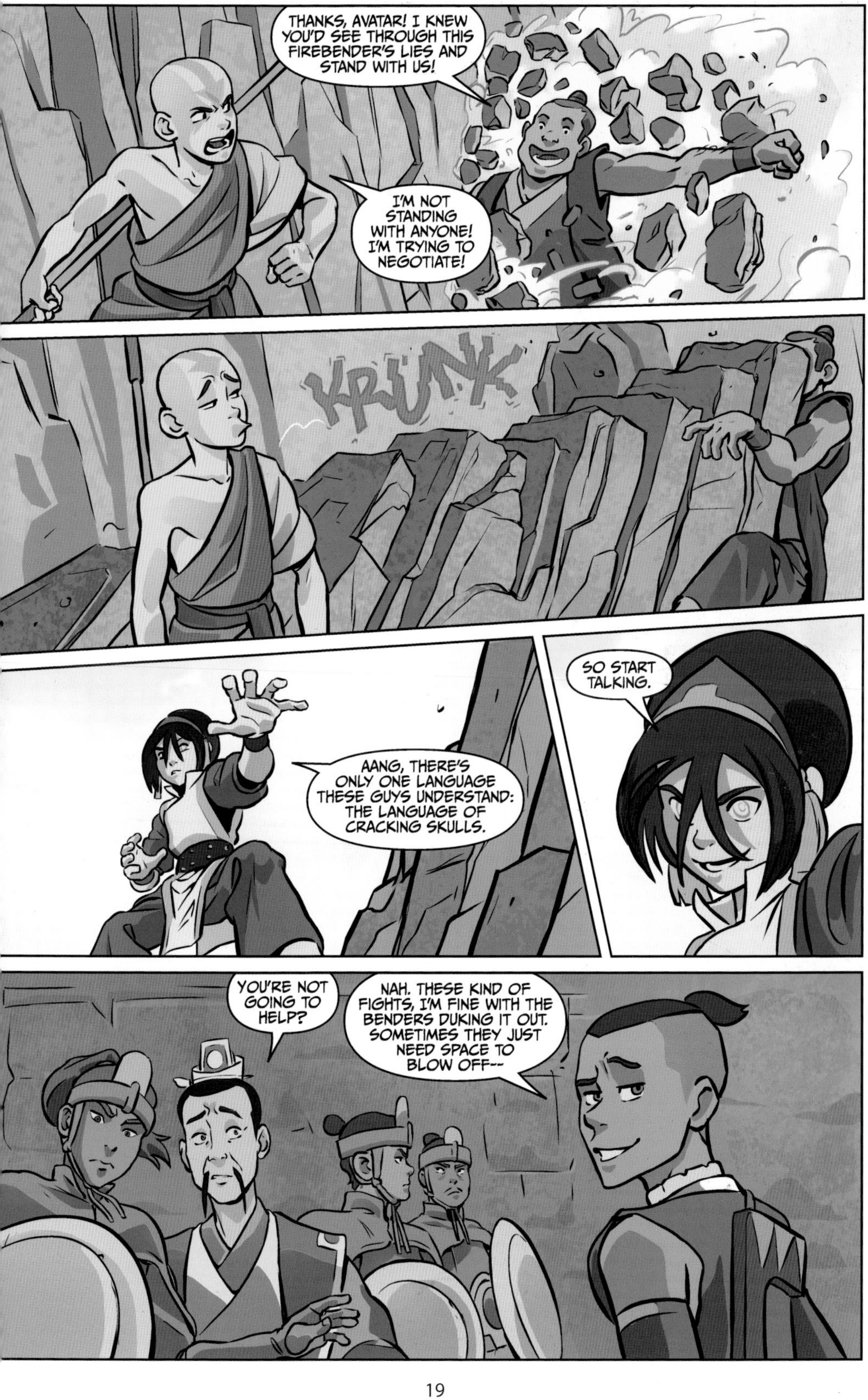
THANKS, AVATAR! I KNEW YOU'D SEE THROUGH THIS FIREBENDER'S LIES AND STAND WITH US!
I'M NOT STANDING WITH ANYONE! I'M TRYING TO NEGOTIATE!
KRUNK
SO START TALKING.
AANG, THERE'S ONLY ONE LANGUAGE THESE GUYS UNDERSTAND: THE LANGUAGE OF CRACKING SKULLS.
YOU'RE NOT GOING TO HELP?
NAH. THESE KIND OF FIGHTS, I'M FINE WITH THE BENDERS DUKING IT OUT. SOMETIMES THEY JUST NEED SPACE TO BLOW OFF--

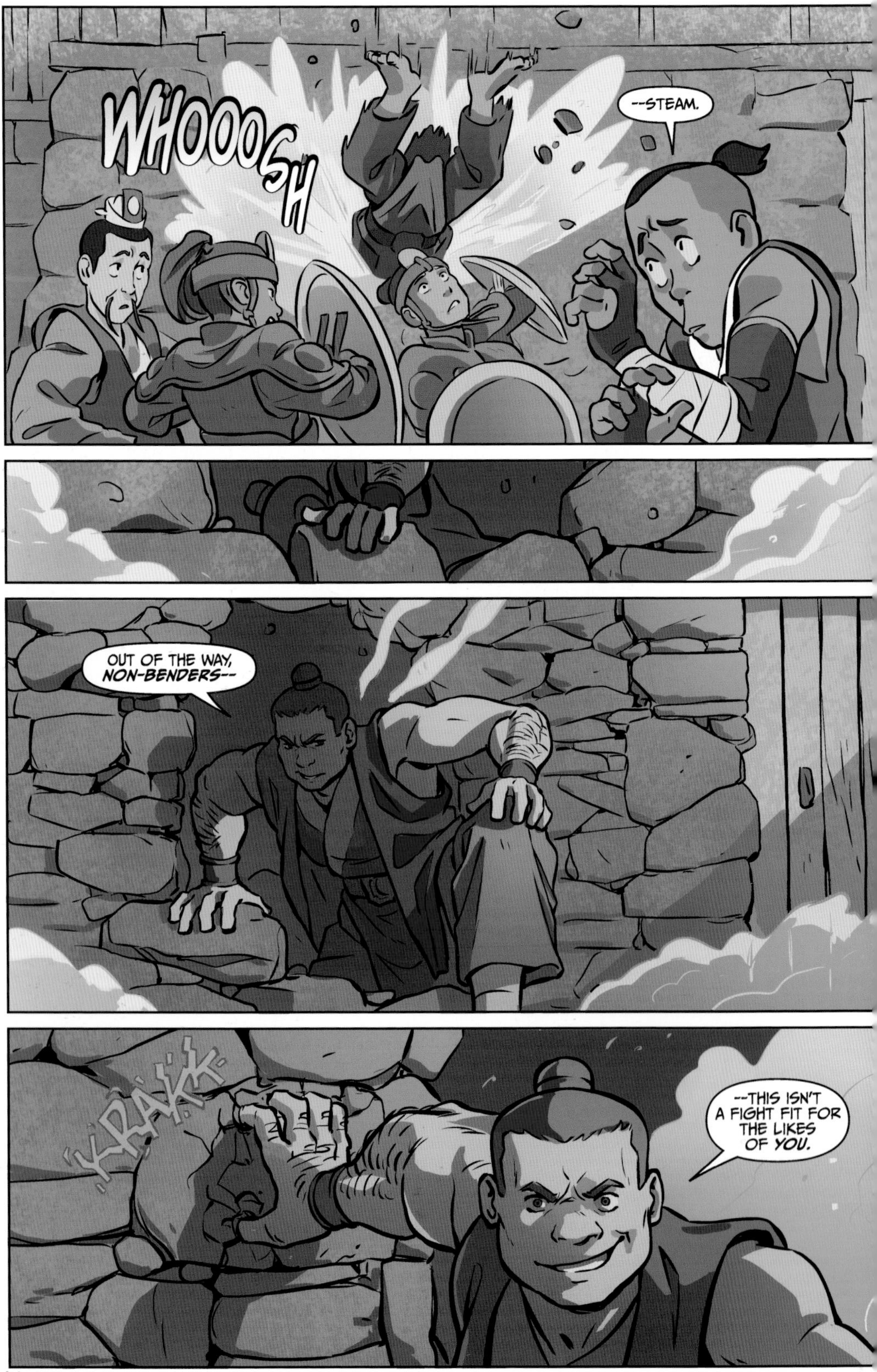
WHOOOOSH
--STEAM.
OUT OF THE WAY, NON-BENDERS--
KRAKK
--THIS ISN'T A FIGHT FIT FOR THE LIKES OF YOU.

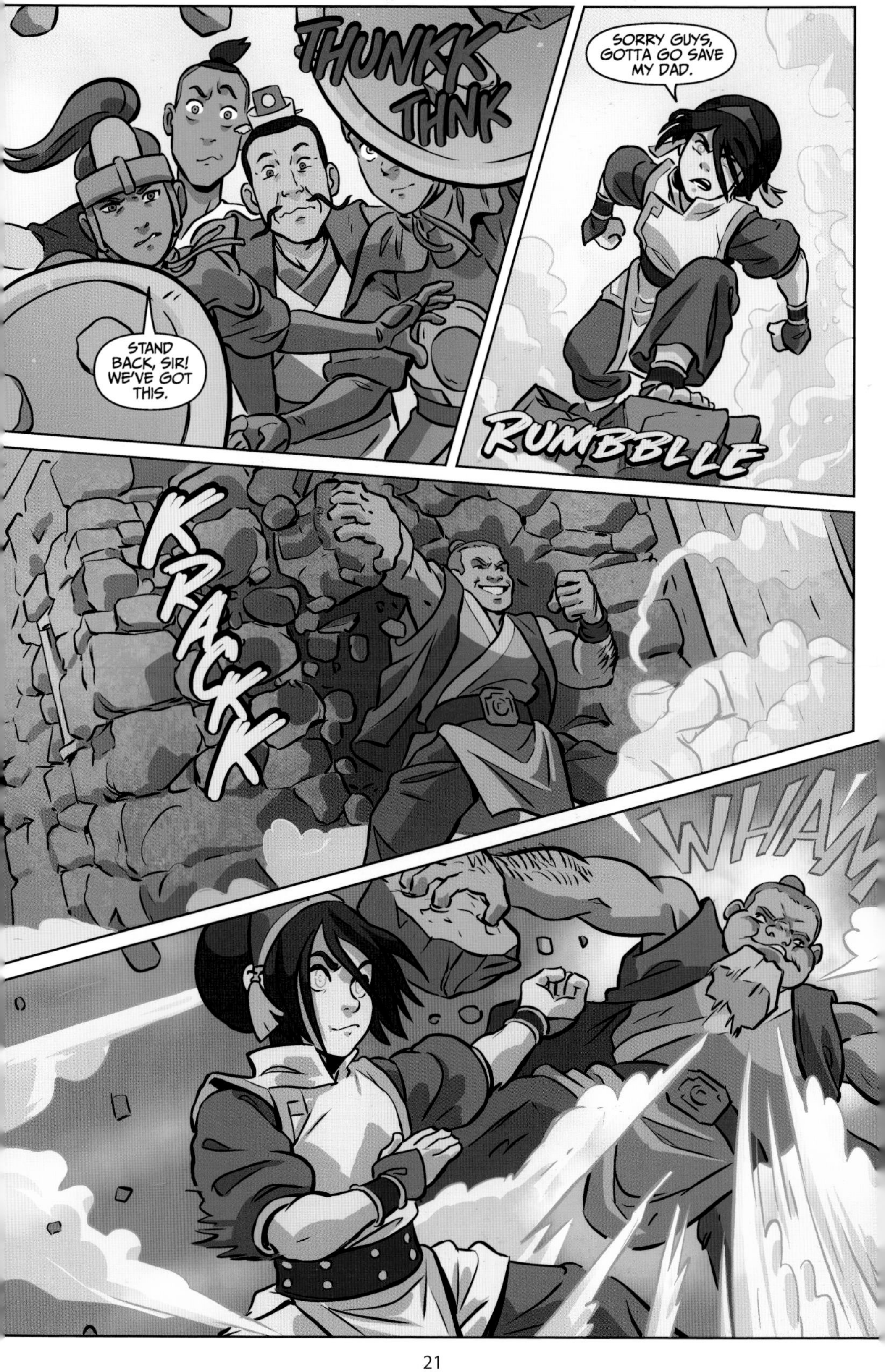
THUNKK
THNK
STAND BACK, SIR! WE'VE GOT THIS.
SORRY GUYS, GOTTA GO SAVE MY DAD.
RUMBBLLE
KRACKK
WHAM

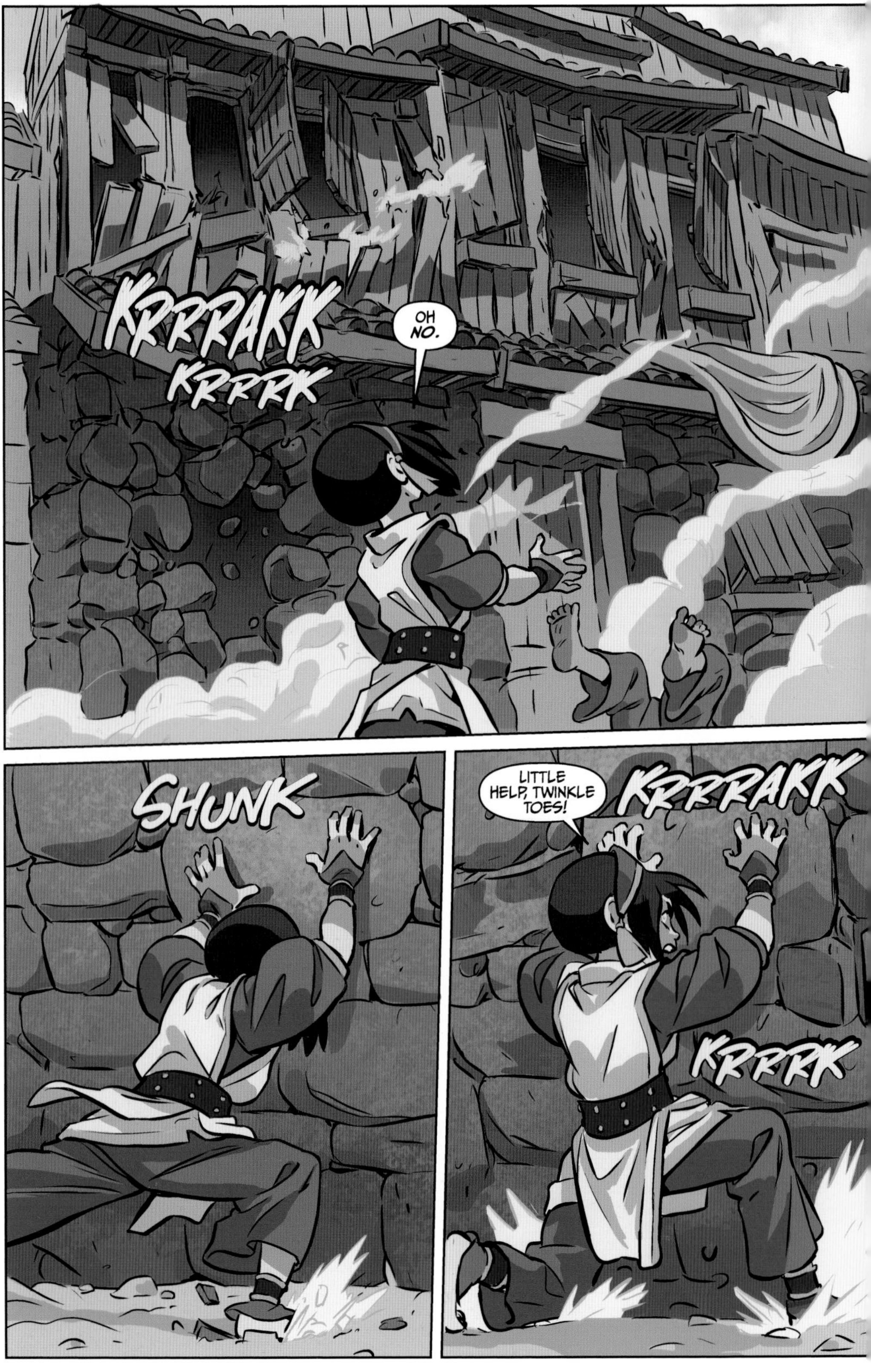
KRRRAKK
KRRRK
OH NO.
SHUNK
LITTLE HELP, TWINKLE TOES!
KRRRAKK
KRRRK

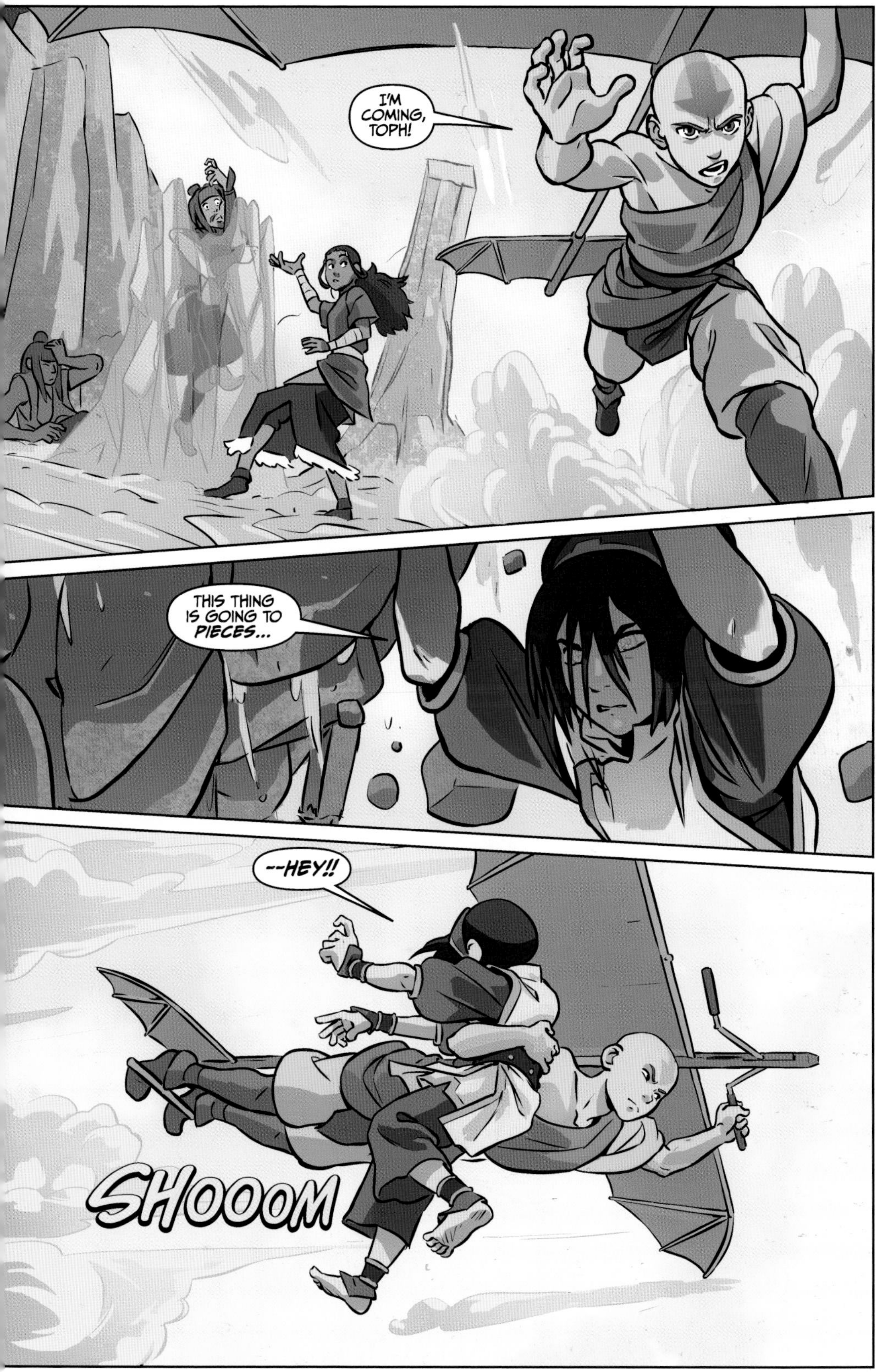
I'M COMING, TOPH!
THIS THING IS GOING TO PIECES...
--HEY!!
SHOOOM

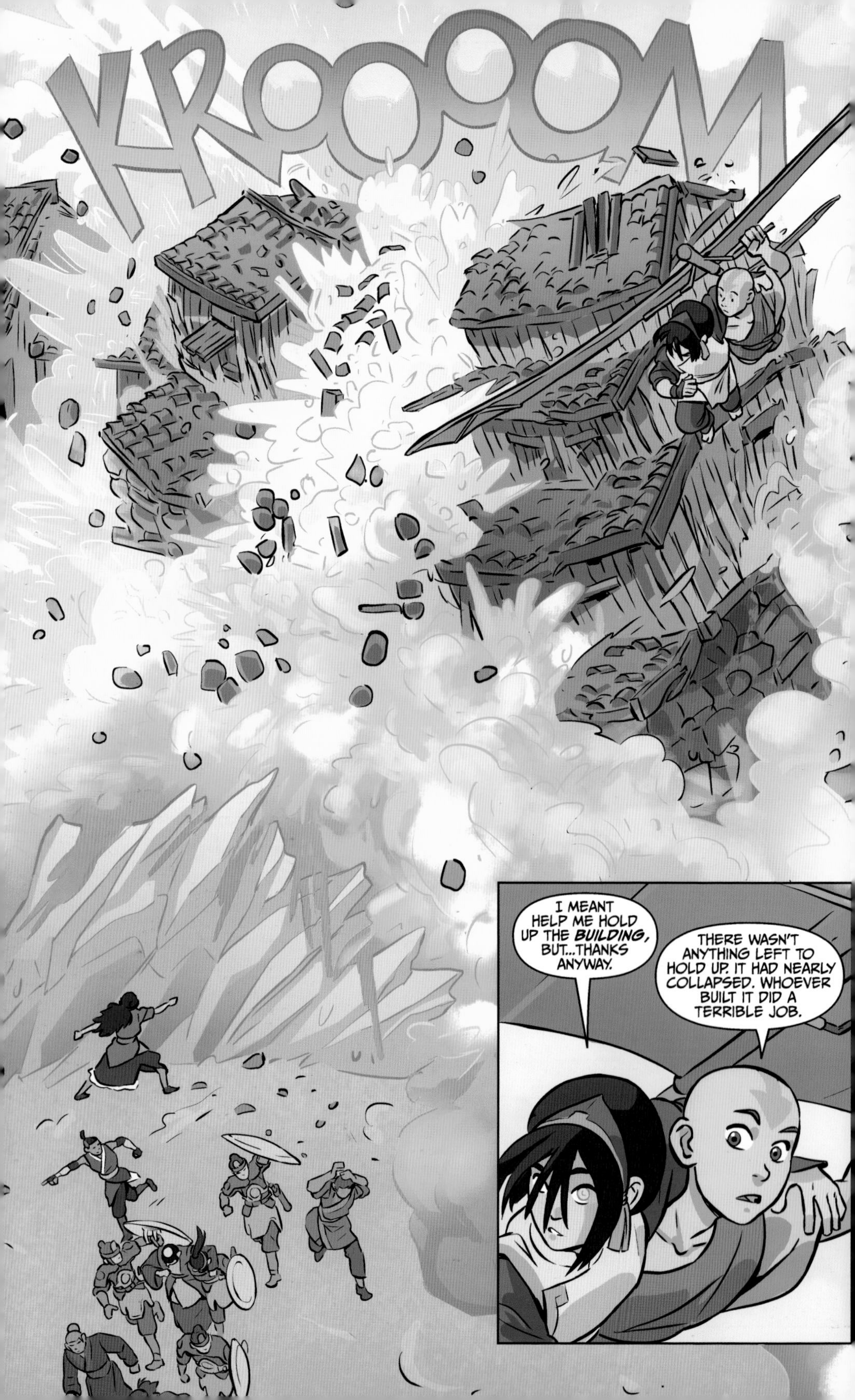
KROOOOM
I MEANT HELP ME HOLD UP THE **BUILDING**, BUT...THANKS ANYWAY.
THERE WASN'T ANYTHING LEFT TO HOLD UP. IT HAD NEARLY COLLAPSED. WHOEVER BUILT IT DID A TERRIBLE JOB.

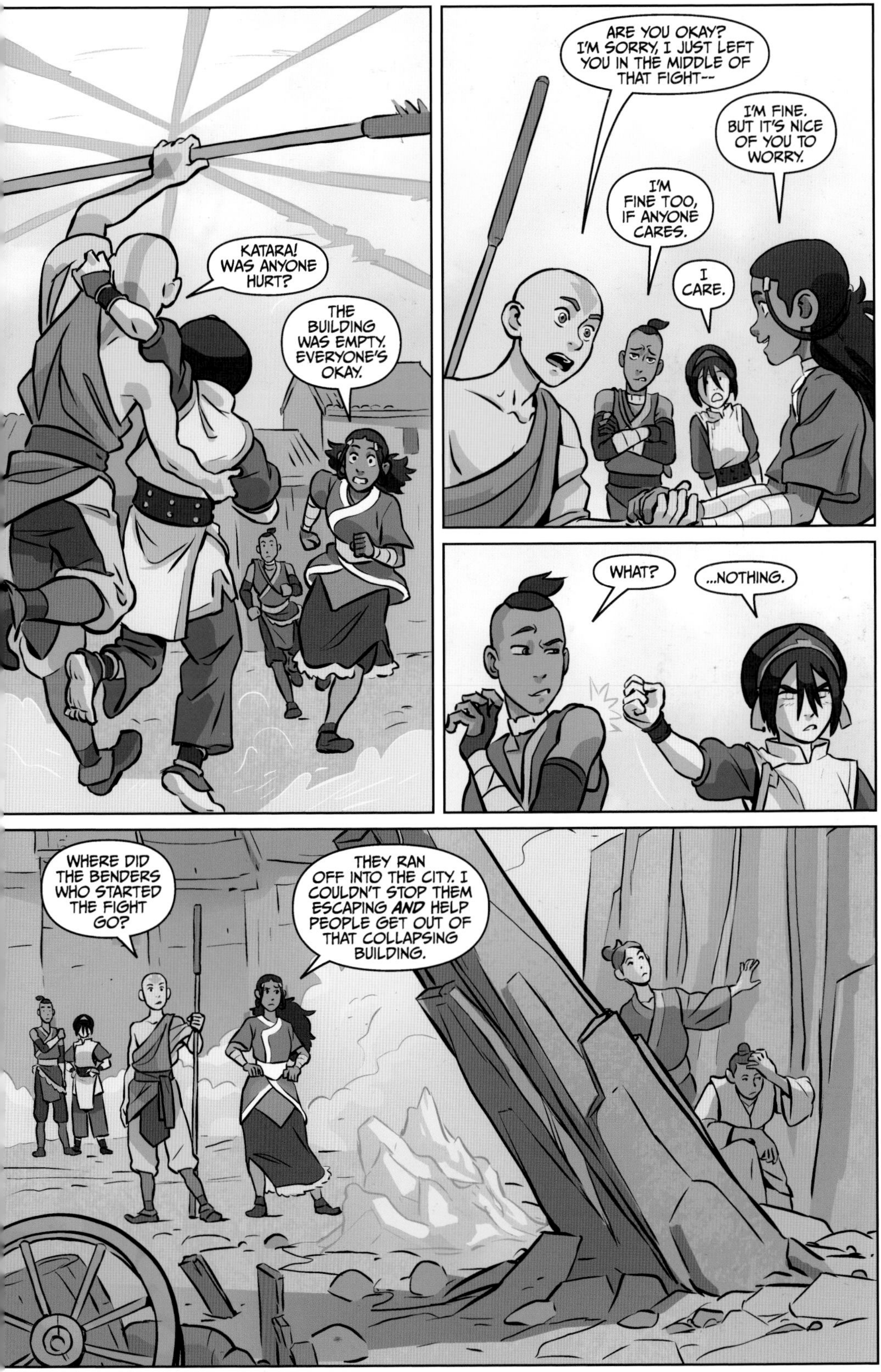
KATARA! WAS ANYONE HURT?
THE BUILDING WAS EMPTY. EVERYONE'S OKAY.
ARE YOU OKAY? I'M SORRY, I JUST LEFT YOU IN THE MIDDLE OF THAT FIGHT--
I'M FINE. BUT IT'S NICE OF YOU TO WORRY.
I'M FINE TOO, IF ANYONE CARES.
I CARE.
WHAT?
...NOTHING.
WHERE DID THE BENDERS WHO STARTED THE FIGHT GO?
THEY RAN OFF INTO THE CITY. I COULDN'T STOP THEM ESCAPING AND HELP PEOPLE GET OUT OF THAT COLLAPSING BUILDING.

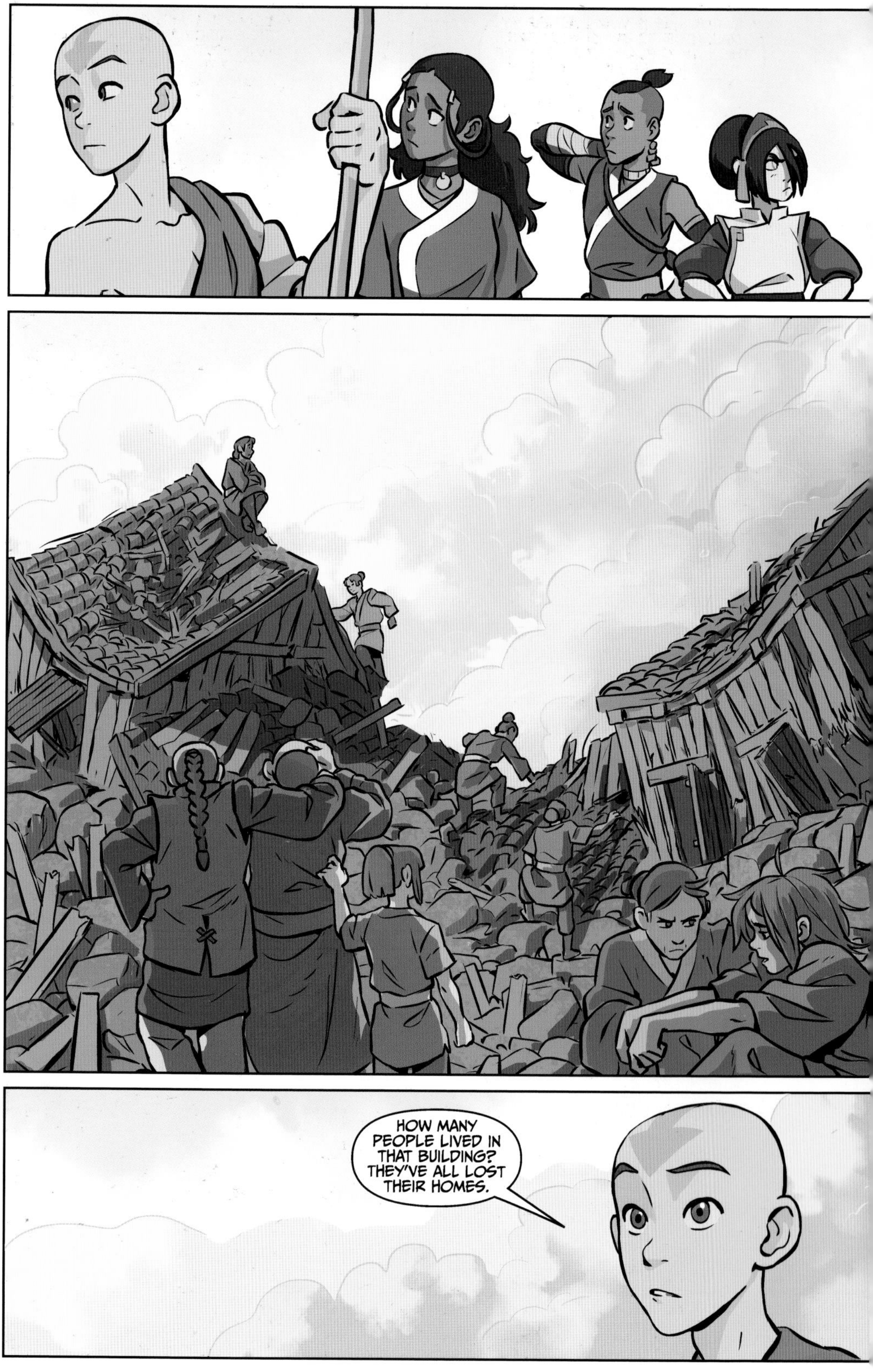
HOW MANY PEOPLE LIVED IN THAT BUILDING? THEY'VE ALL LOST THEIR HOMES.

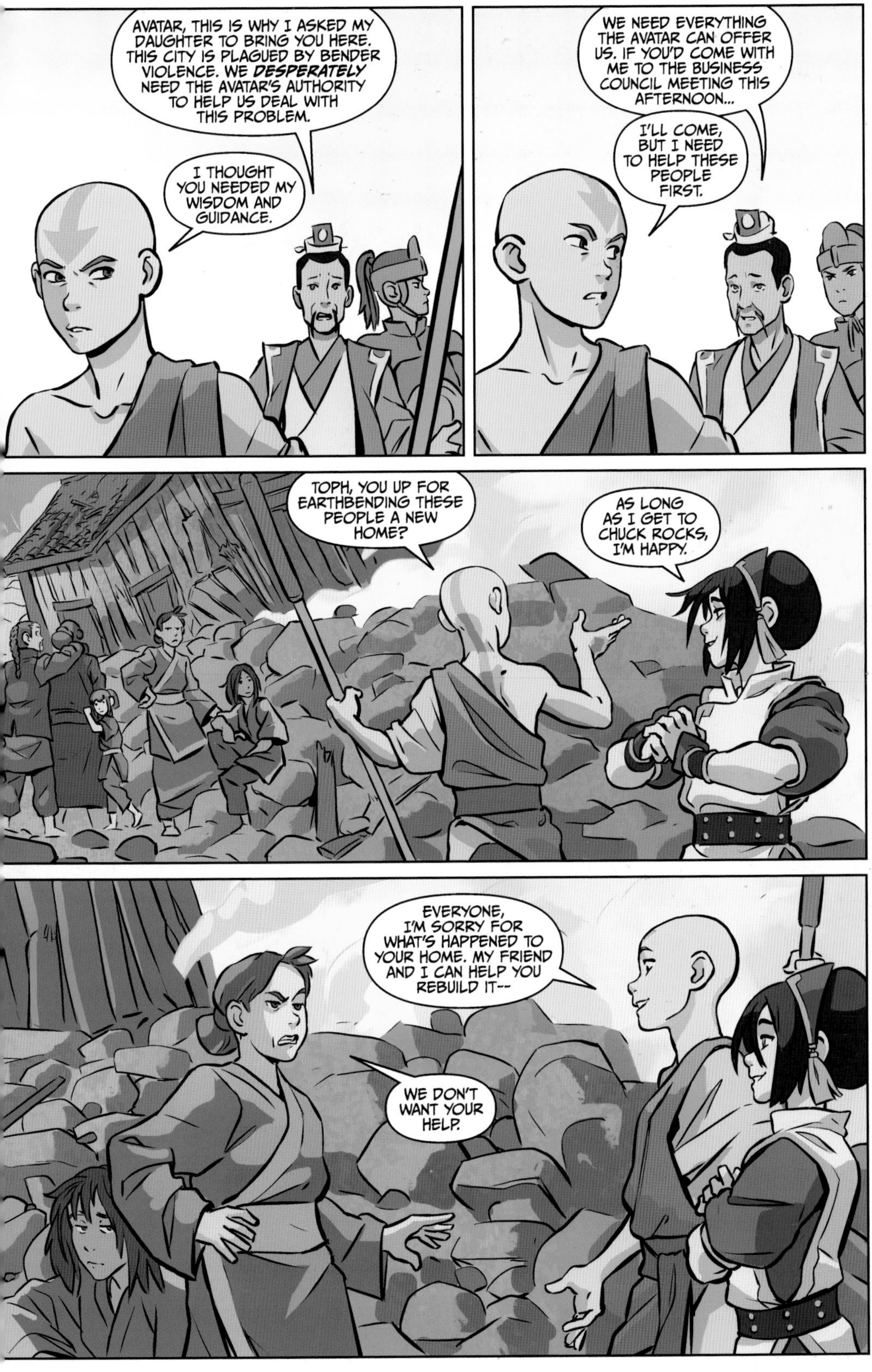
AVATAR, THIS IS WHY I ASKED MY DAUGHTER TO BRING YOU HERE. THIS CITY IS PLAGUED BY BENDER VIOLENCE. WE *DESPERATELY* NEED THE AVATAR'S AUTHORITY TO HELP US DEAL WITH THIS PROBLEM.
I THOUGHT YOU NEEDED MY WISDOM AND GUIDANCE.
WE NEED EVERYTHING THE AVATAR CAN OFFER US. IF YOU'D COME WITH ME TO THE BUSINESS COUNCIL MEETING THIS AFTERNOON...
I'LL COME, BUT I NEED TO HELP THESE PEOPLE FIRST.
TOPH, YOU UP FOR EARTHBENDING THESE PEOPLE A NEW HOME?
AS LONG AS I GET TO CHUCK ROCKS, I'M HAPPY.
EVERYONE, I'M SORRY FOR WHAT'S HAPPENED TO YOUR HOME. MY FRIEND AND I CAN HELP YOU REBUILD IT--
WE DON'T WANT YOUR HELP.

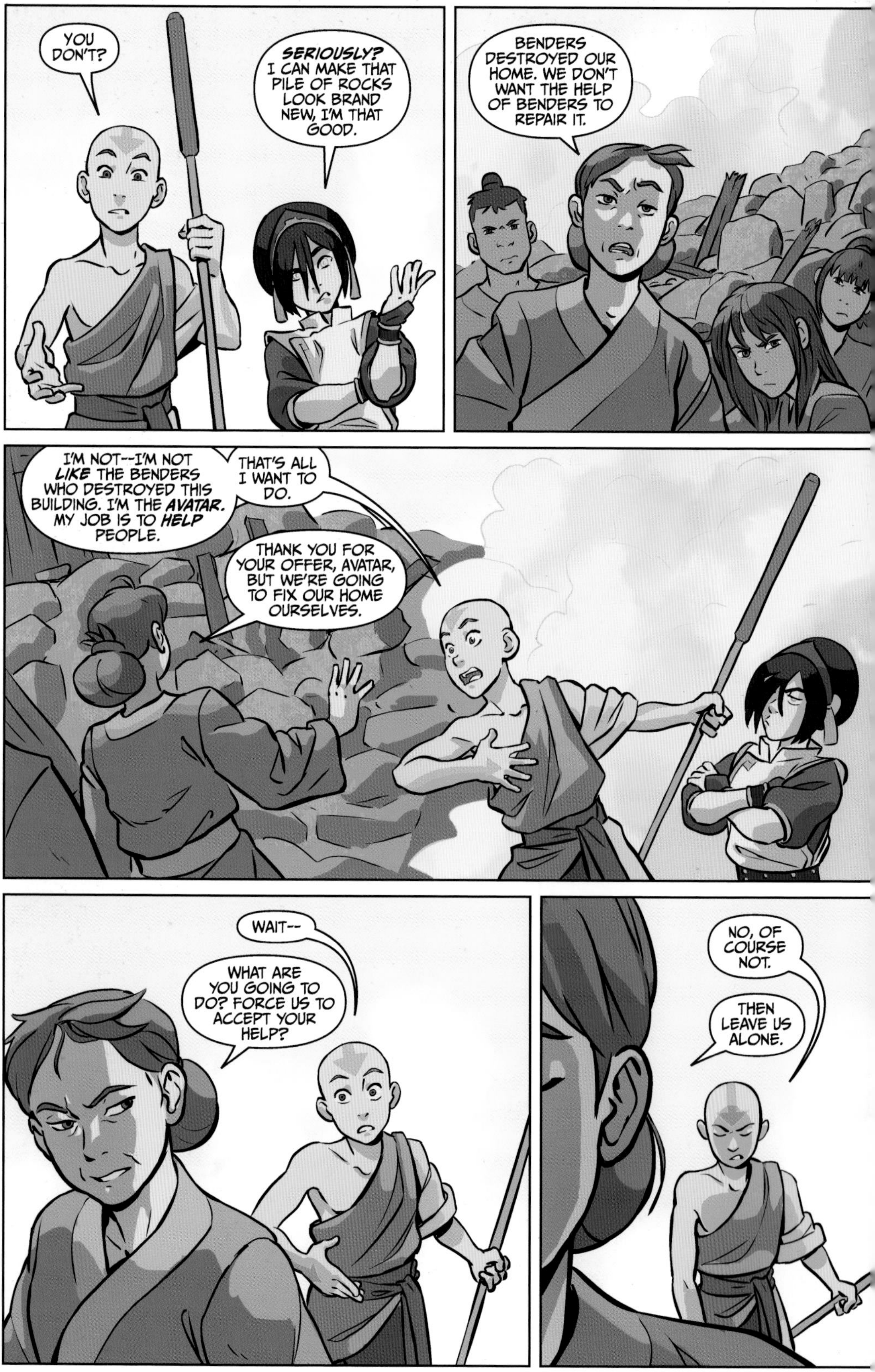
YOU DON'T?
SERIOUSLY? I CAN MAKE THAT PILE OF ROCKS LOOK BRAND NEW, I'M THAT GOOD.
BENDERS DESTROYED OUR HOME. WE DON'T WANT THE HELP OF BENDERS TO REPAIR IT.
I'M NOT--I'M NOT LIKE THE BENDERS WHO DESTROYED THIS BUILDING. I'M THE AVATAR. MY JOB IS TO HELP PEOPLE.
THAT'S ALL I WANT TO DO.
THANK YOU FOR YOUR OFFER, AVATAR, BUT WE'RE GOING TO FIX OUR HOME OURSELVES.
WAIT--
WHAT ARE YOU GOING TO DO? FORCE US TO ACCEPT YOUR HELP?
NO, OF COURSE NOT.
THEN LEAVE US ALONE.

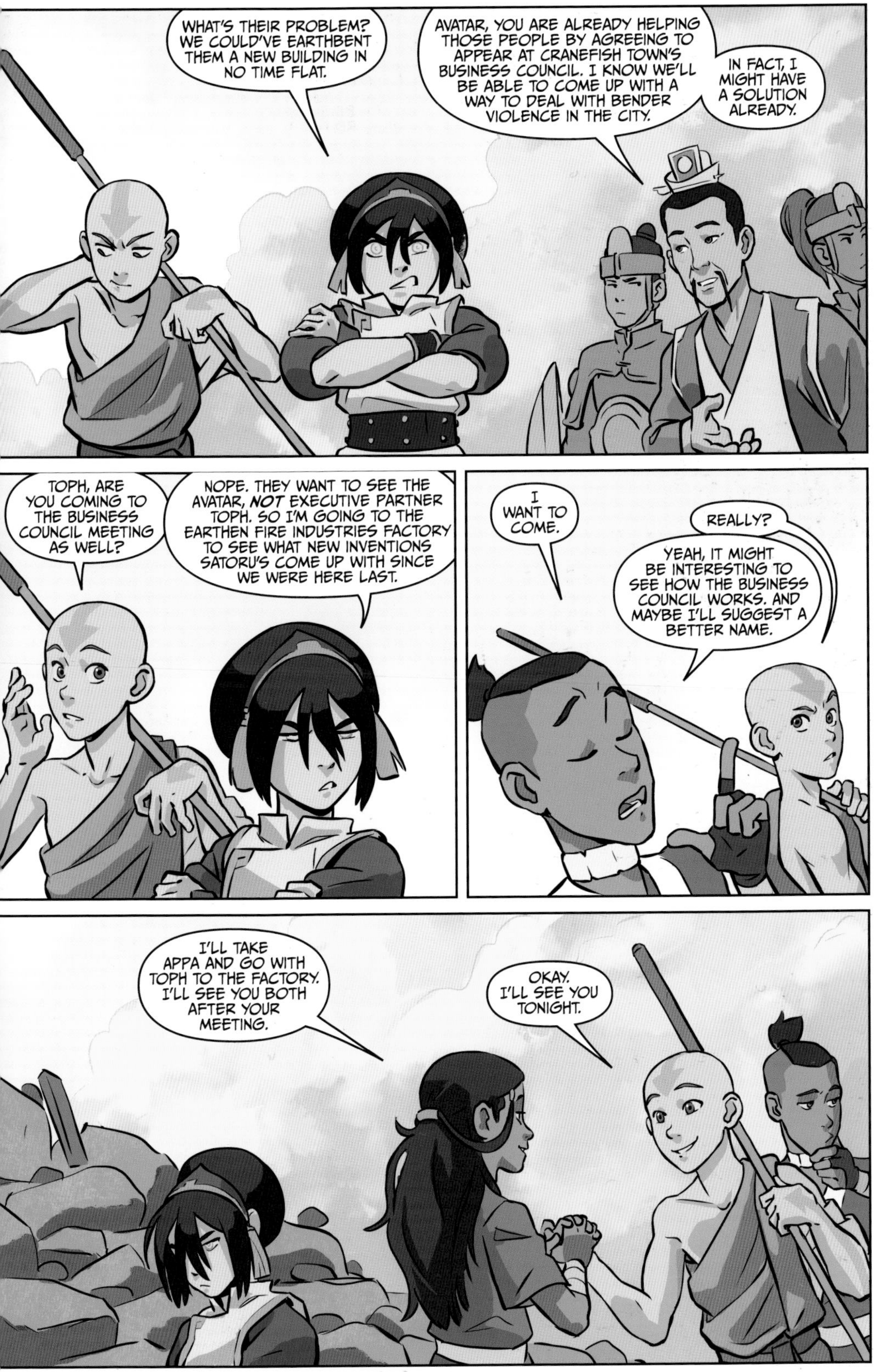
WHAT'S THEIR PROBLEM? WE COULD'VE EARTHBENT THEM A NEW BUILDING IN NO TIME FLAT.
AVATAR, YOU ARE ALREADY HELPING THOSE PEOPLE BY AGREEING TO APPEAR AT CRANEFISH TOWN'S BUSINESS COUNCIL. I KNOW WE'LL BE ABLE TO COME UP WITH A WAY TO DEAL WITH BENDER VIOLENCE IN THE CITY.
IN FACT, I MIGHT HAVE A SOLUTION ALREADY.
TOPH, ARE YOU COMING TO THE BUSINESS COUNCIL MEETING AS WELL?
NOPE. THEY WANT TO SEE THE AVATAR, *NOT* EXECUTIVE PARTNER TOPH. SO I'M GOING TO THE EARTHEN FIRE INDUSTRIES FACTORY TO SEE WHAT NEW INVENTIONS SATORU'S COME UP WITH SINCE WE WERE HERE LAST.
I WANT TO COME.
REALLY?
YEAH, IT MIGHT BE INTERESTING TO SEE HOW THE BUSINESS COUNCIL WORKS. AND MAYBE I'LL SUGGEST A BETTER NAME.
I'LL TAKE APPA AND GO WITH TOPH TO THE FACTORY. I'LL SEE YOU BOTH AFTER YOUR MEETING.
OKAY. I'LL SEE YOU TONIGHT.

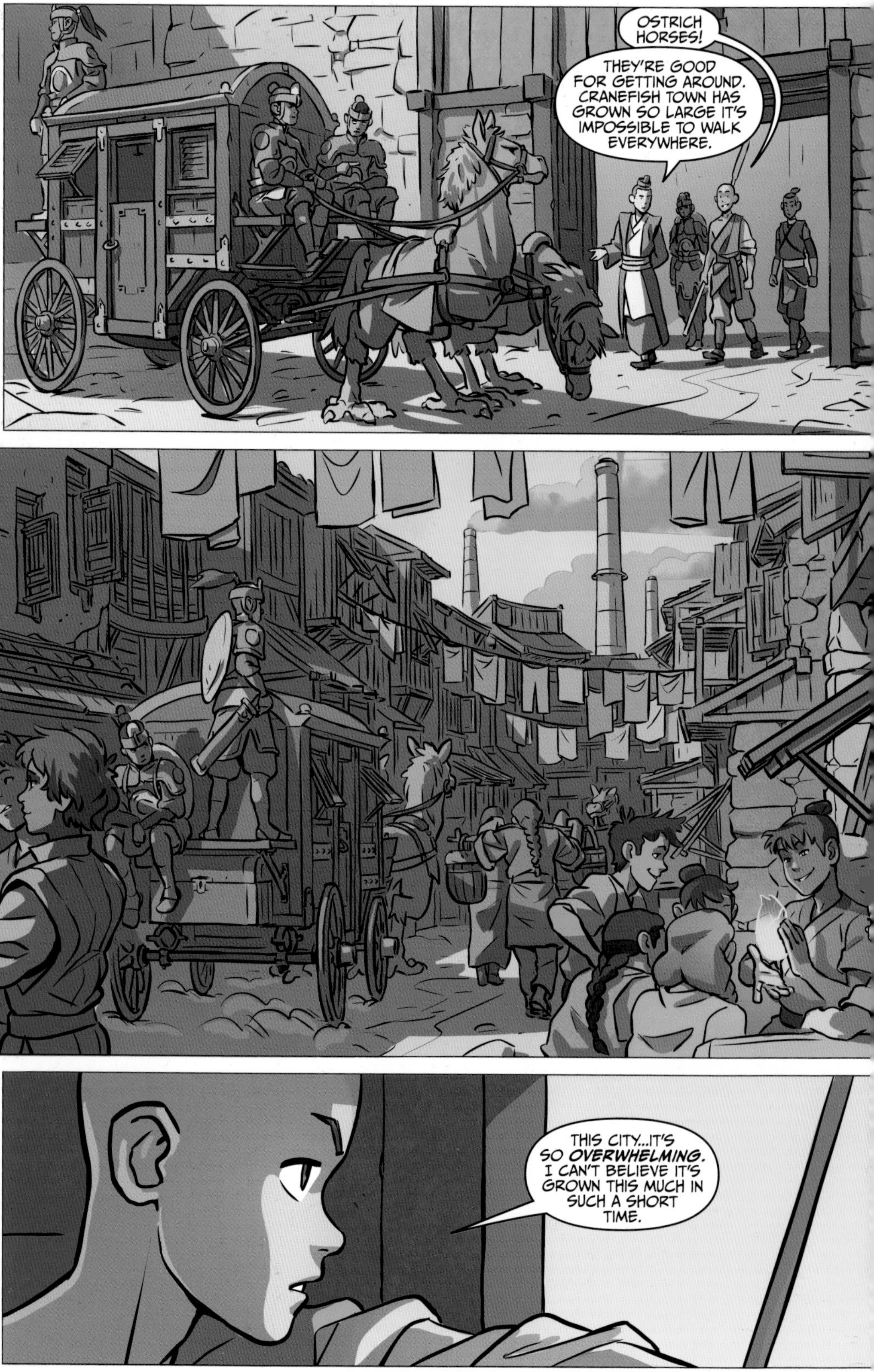
OSTRICH HORSES!
THEY'RE GOOD FOR GETTING AROUND. CRANEFISH TOWN HAS GROWN SO LARGE IT'S IMPOSSIBLE TO WALK EVERYWHERE.
THIS CITY...IT'S SO OVERWHELMING. I CAN'T BELIEVE IT'S GROWN THIS MUCH IN SUCH A SHORT TIME.

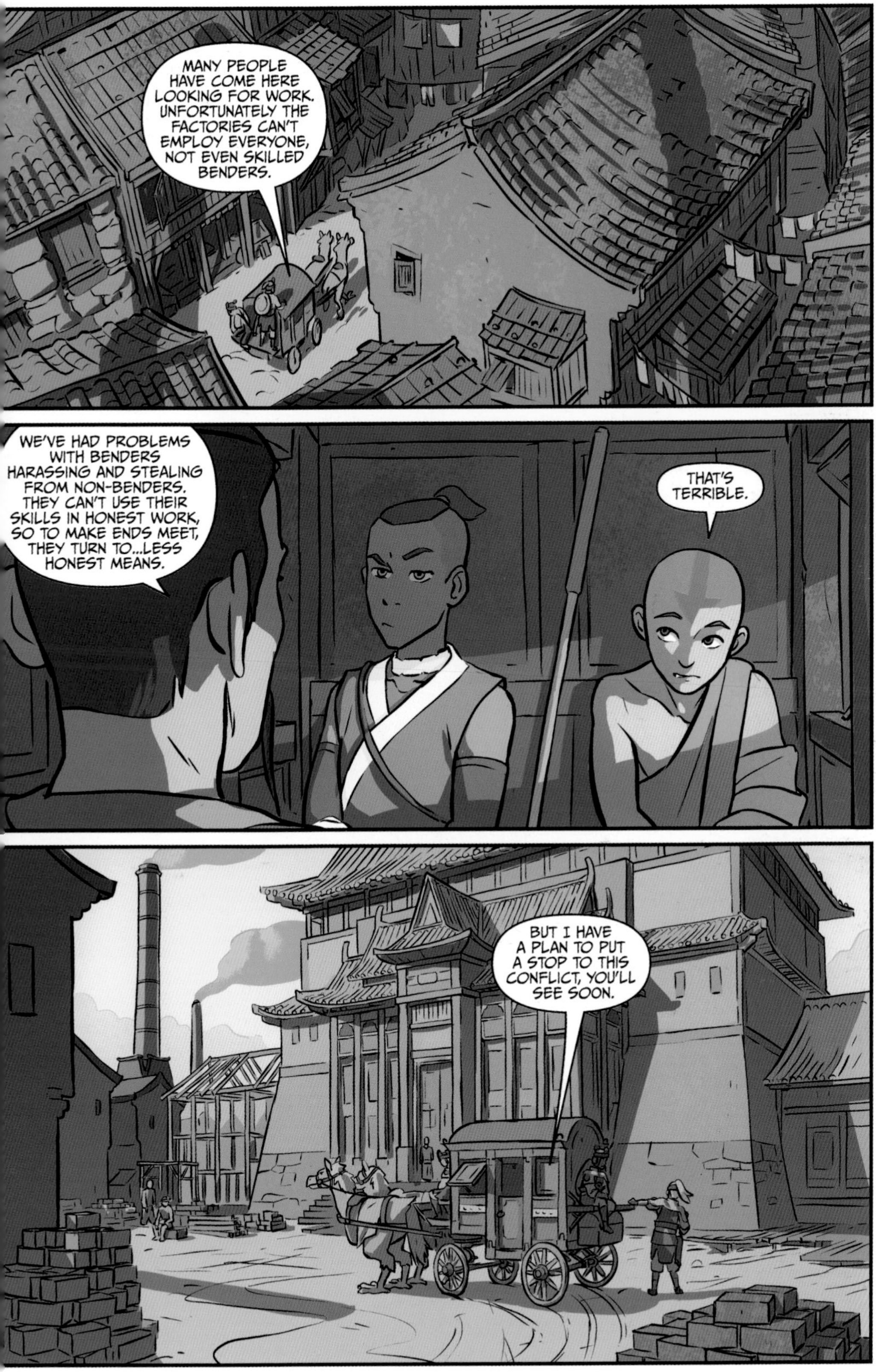
MANY PEOPLE HAVE COME HERE LOOKING FOR WORK. UNFORTUNATELY THE FACTORIES CAN'T EMPLOY EVERYONE, NOT EVEN SKILLED BENDERS.
WE'VE HAD PROBLEMS WITH BENDERS HARASSING AND STEALING FROM NON-BENDERS. THEY CAN'T USE THEIR SKILLS IN HONEST WORK, SO TO MAKE ENDS MEET, THEY TURN TO...LESS HONEST MEANS.
THAT'S TERRIBLE.
BUT I HAVE A PLAN TO PUT A STOP TO THIS CONFLICT, YOU'LL SEE SOON.

GOOD AFTERNOON, FELLOW COUNCIL MEMBERS.

WE THOUGHT YOU MIGHT NOT BE COMING. BETTER LATE THAN NEVER.

LAO, GOOD OF YOU TO JOIN US.

COUNCILMAN LAO HAS ATTENDED EVERY BUSINESS COUNCIL MEETING. THERE WAS NO REASON TO THINK HE WOULDN'T BE HERE TODAY.

YOU WERE JUST LOOKING FOR A REASON TO START WITHOUT HIM.

I WAS DELAYED, BUT I HAVE SOME GOOD NEWS.

AANG, YOU NOTICE SOMETHING ABOUT THE PEOPLE ON THIS BUSINESS COUNCIL?

NOTICE WHAT?

LOOK AT THEM.

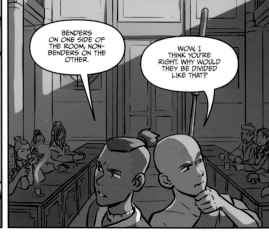

BENDERS ON ONE SIDE OF THE ROOM, NON-BENDERS ON THE OTHER.

WOW, I THINK YOU'RE RIGHT. WHY WOULD THEY BE DIVIDED LIKE THAT?

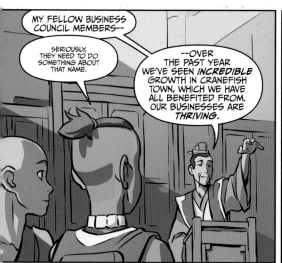

MY FELLOW BUSINESS COUNCIL MEMBERS--

SERIOUSLY, THEY NEED TO DO SOMETHING ABOUT THAT NAME.

--OVER THE PAST YEAR WE'VE SEEN *INCREDIBLE* GROWTH IN CRANEFISH TOWN, WHICH WE HAVE ALL BENEFITED FROM. OUR BUSINESSES ARE *THRIVING.*

HOWEVER, OUR CITY'S GROWTH HAS ALSO BROUGHT... *CHALLENGES.*

OUR HOME IS PLAGUED BY VIOLENCE, ESPECIALLY *BENDER* VIOLENCE. OUR FACTORY EMPLOYEES ARE AFRAID TO WALK TO WORK FOR FEAR OF BEING ATTACKED.

I WANT TO PROPOSE SOMETHING. *WE* ARE CRANEFISH TOWN'S COMMUNITY LEADERS. IT'S UP TO *US* TO FIND A WAY TO DEAL WITH THE ISSUES OUR CITY IS FACING.

I PROPOSE THAT BENDING BE *BANNED* ON PUBLIC STREETS. THIS WILL HELP PREVENT THE BENDER VIOLENCE THAT IS CAUSING SO MANY PROBLEMS.

BAN BENDING...?

33

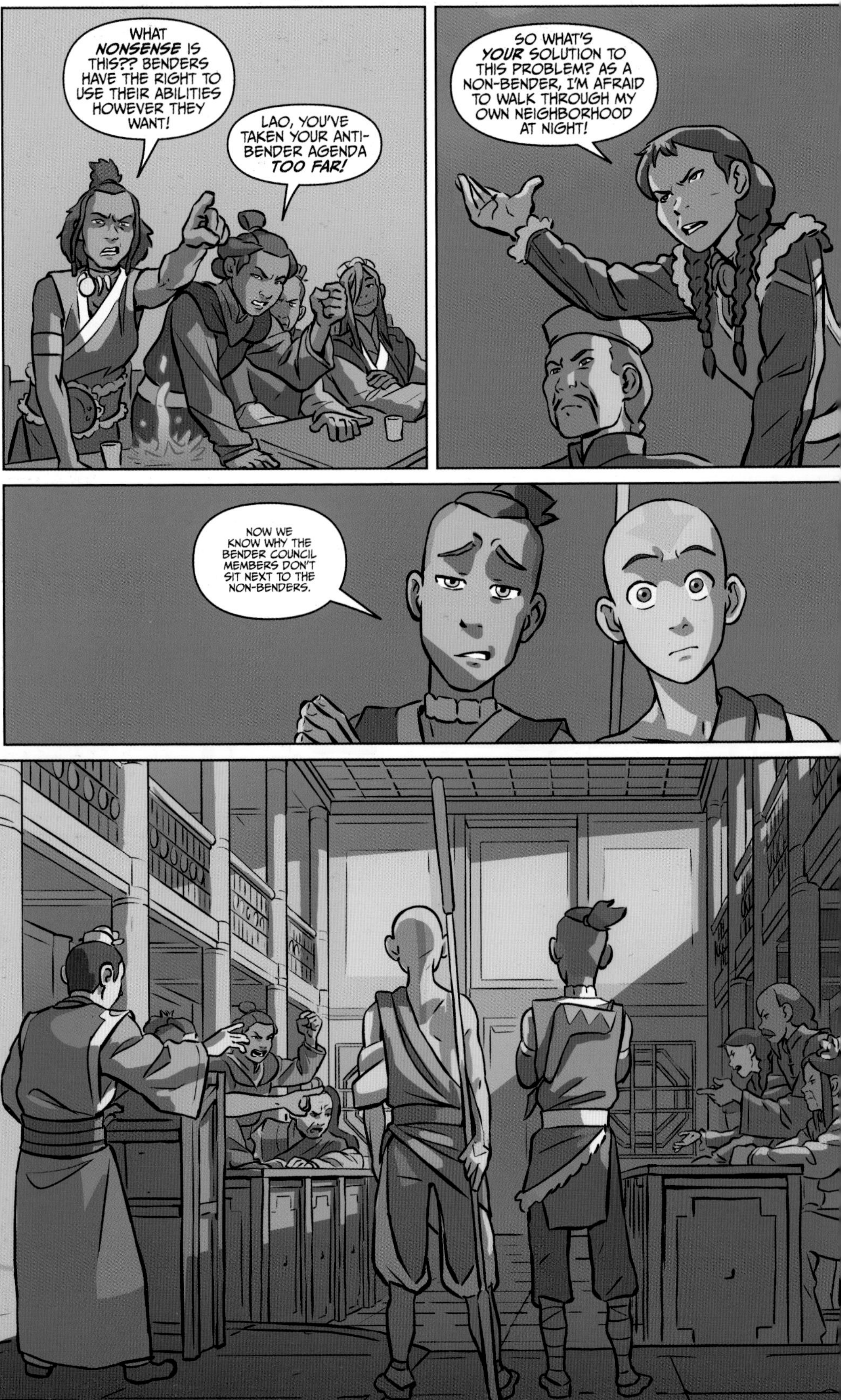
WHAT NONSENSE IS THIS?? BENDERS HAVE THE RIGHT TO USE THEIR ABILITIES HOWEVER THEY WANT!
LAO, YOU'VE TAKEN YOUR ANTI-BENDER AGENDA TOO FAR!
SO WHAT'S YOUR SOLUTION TO THIS PROBLEM? AS A NON-BENDER, I'M AFRAID TO WALK THROUGH MY OWN NEIGHBORHOOD AT NIGHT!
NOW WE KNOW WHY THE BENDER COUNCIL MEMBERS DON'T SIT NEXT TO THE NON-BENDERS.

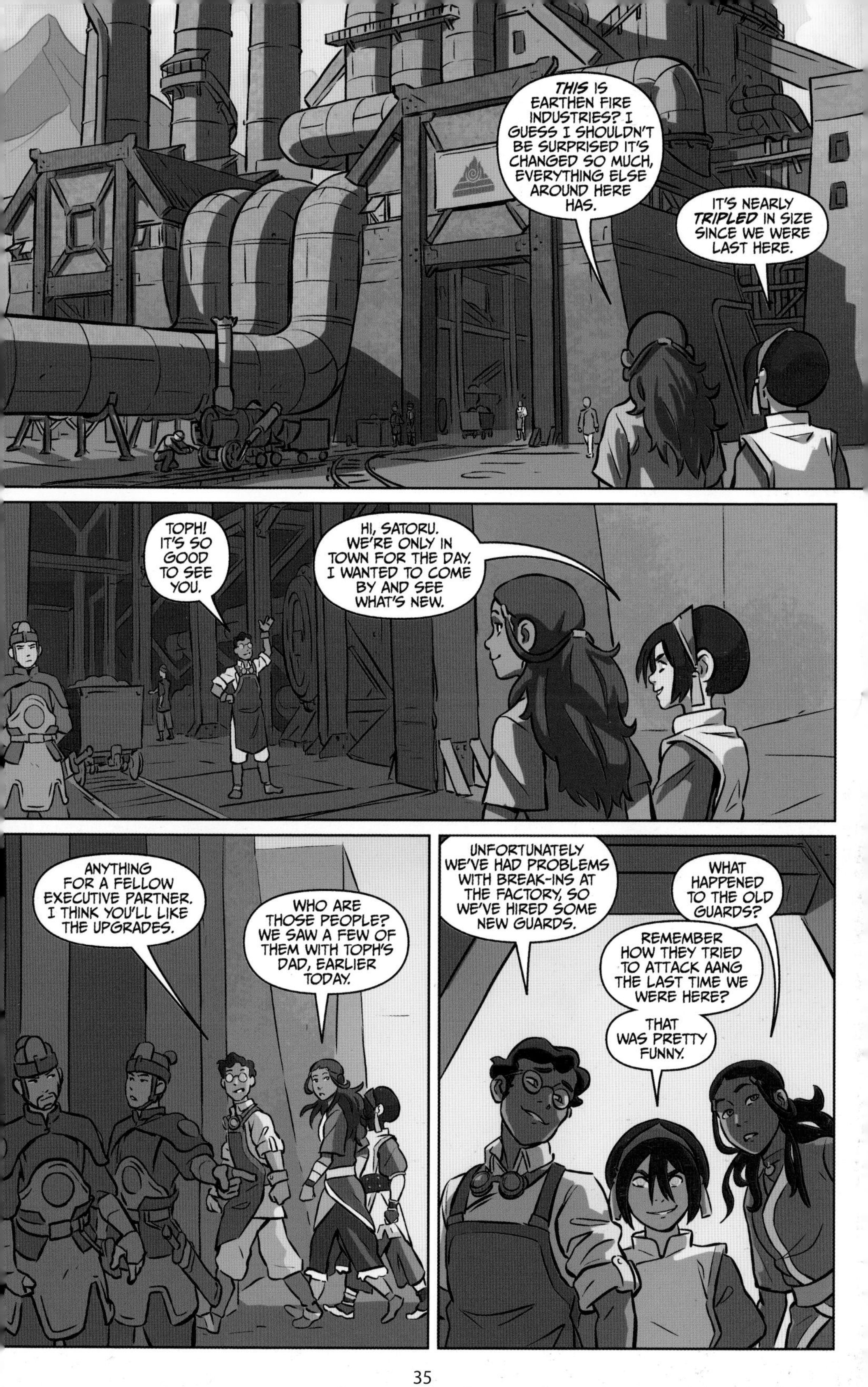
THIS IS EARTHEN FIRE INDUSTRIES? I GUESS I SHOULDN'T BE SURPRISED IT'S CHANGED SO MUCH, EVERYTHING ELSE AROUND HERE HAS.
IT'S NEARLY TRIPLED IN SIZE SINCE WE WERE LAST HERE.
TOPH! IT'S SO GOOD TO SEE YOU.
HI, SATORU. WE'RE ONLY IN TOWN FOR THE DAY. I WANTED TO COME BY AND SEE WHAT'S NEW.
ANYTHING FOR A FELLOW EXECUTIVE PARTNER. I THINK YOU'LL LIKE THE UPGRADES.
WHO ARE THOSE PEOPLE? WE SAW A FEW OF THEM WITH TOPH'S DAD, EARLIER TODAY.
UNFORTUNATELY WE'VE HAD PROBLEMS WITH BREAK-INS AT THE FACTORY, SO WE'VE HIRED SOME NEW GUARDS.
WHAT HAPPENED TO THE OLD GUARDS?
REMEMBER HOW THEY TRIED TO ATTACK AANG THE LAST TIME WE WERE HERE?
THAT WAS PRETTY FUNNY.

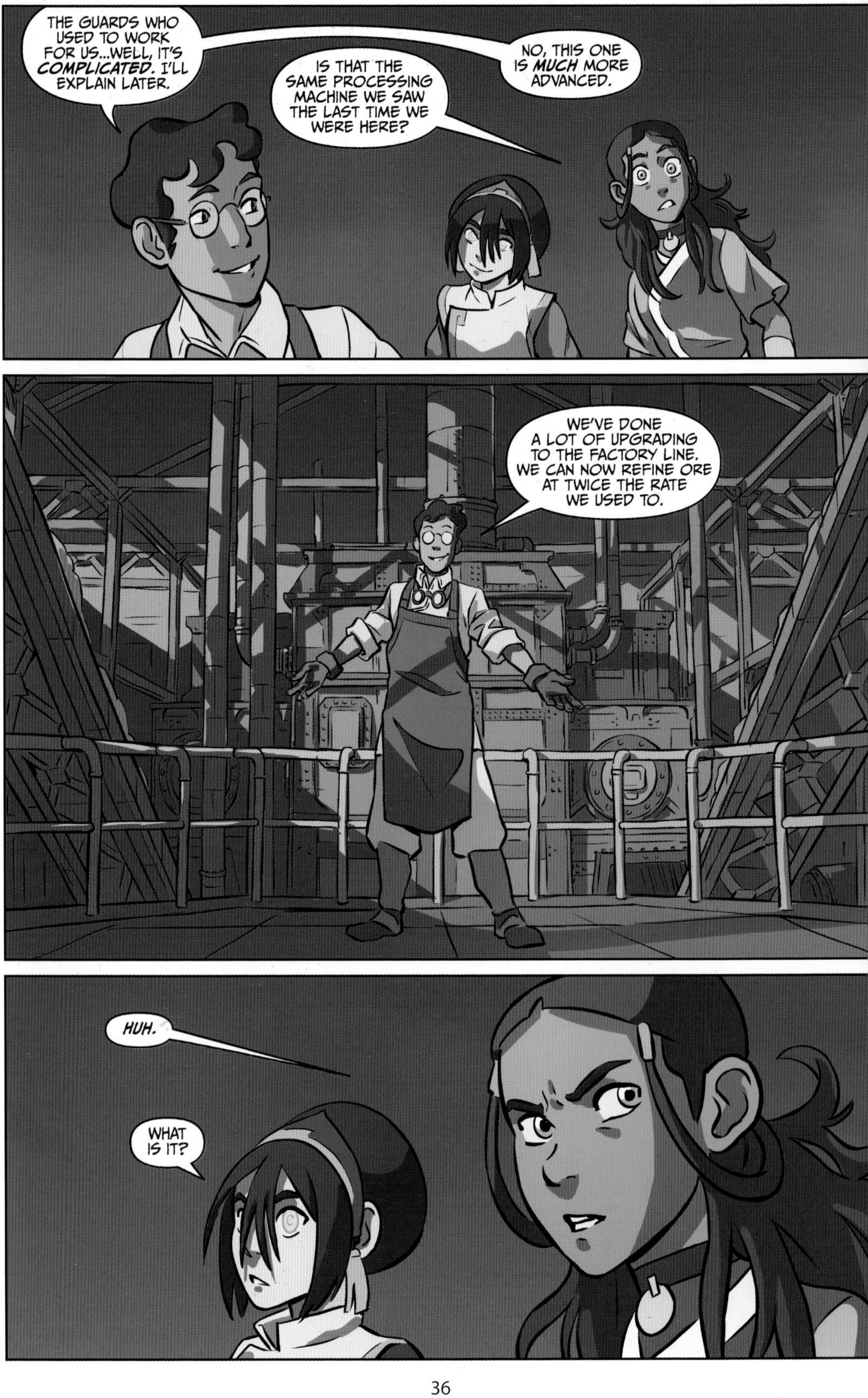
THE GUARDS WHO USED TO WORK FOR US...WELL, IT'S COMPLICATED. I'LL EXPLAIN LATER.
IS THAT THE SAME PROCESSING MACHINE WE SAW THE LAST TIME WE WERE HERE?
NO, THIS ONE IS MUCH MORE ADVANCED.
WE'VE DONE A LOT OF UPGRADING TO THE FACTORY LINE. WE CAN NOW REFINE ORE AT TWICE THE RATE WE USED TO.
HUH.
WHAT IS IT?

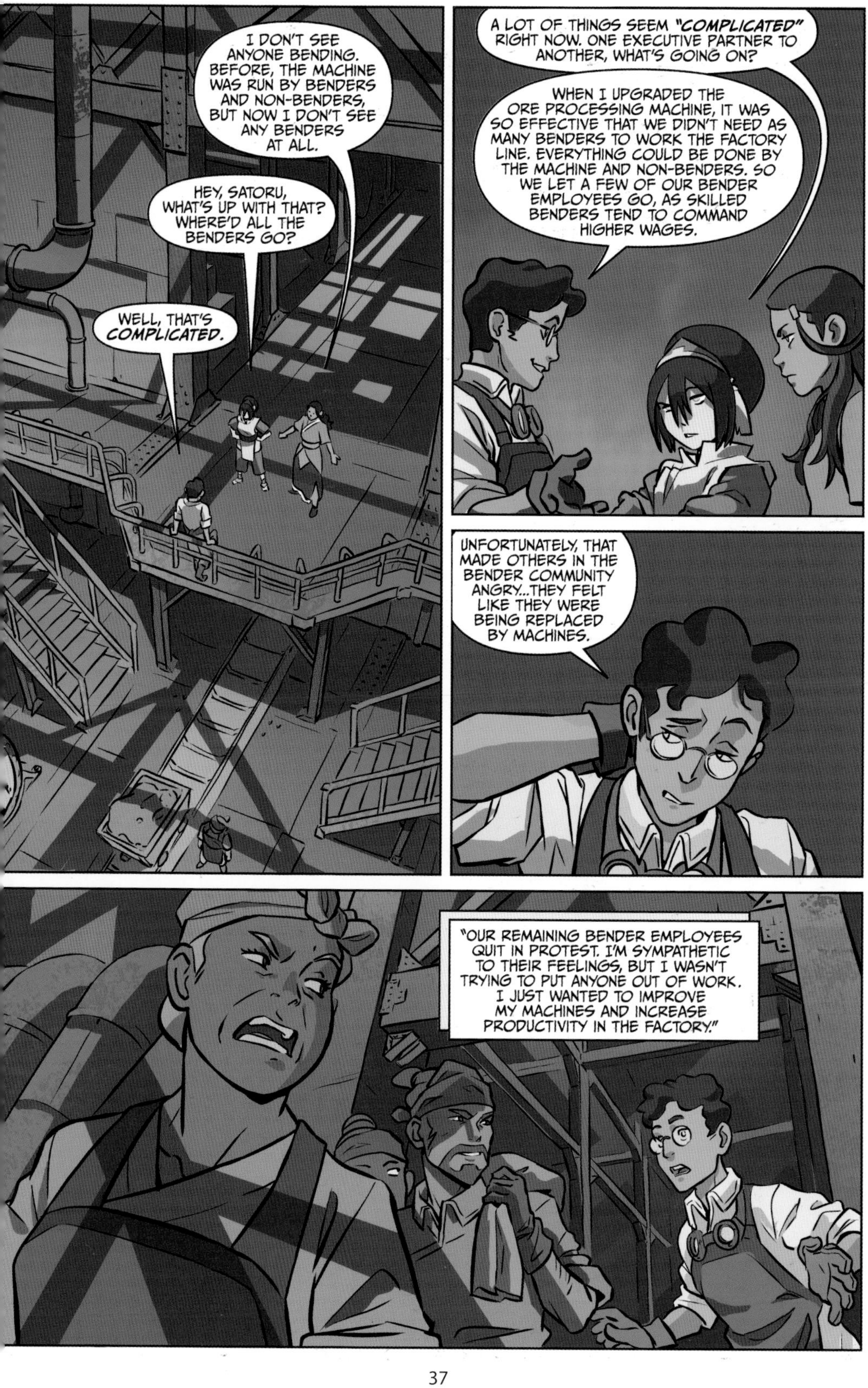
I DON'T SEE ANYONE BENDING. BEFORE, THE MACHINE WAS RUN BY BENDERS AND NON-BENDERS, BUT NOW I DON'T SEE ANY BENDERS AT ALL.
HEY, SATORU, WHAT'S UP WITH THAT? WHERE'D ALL THE BENDERS GO?
WELL, THAT'S *COMPLICATED.*
A LOT OF THINGS SEEM *"COMPLICATED"* RIGHT NOW. ONE EXECUTIVE PARTNER TO ANOTHER, WHAT'S GOING ON?
WHEN I UPGRADED THE ORE PROCESSING MACHINE, IT WAS SO EFFECTIVE THAT WE DIDN'T NEED AS MANY BENDERS TO WORK THE FACTORY LINE. EVERYTHING COULD BE DONE BY THE MACHINE AND NON-BENDERS. SO WE LET A FEW OF OUR BENDER EMPLOYEES GO, AS SKILLED BENDERS TEND TO COMMAND HIGHER WAGES.
UNFORTUNATELY, THAT MADE OTHERS IN THE BENDER COMMUNITY ANGRY...THEY FELT LIKE THEY WERE BEING REPLACED BY MACHINES.
"OUR REMAINING BENDER EMPLOYEES QUIT IN PROTEST. I'M SYMPATHETIC TO THEIR FEELINGS, BUT I WASN'T TRYING TO PUT ANYONE OUT OF WORK. I JUST WANTED TO IMPROVE MY MACHINES AND INCREASE PRODUCTIVITY IN THE FACTORY."

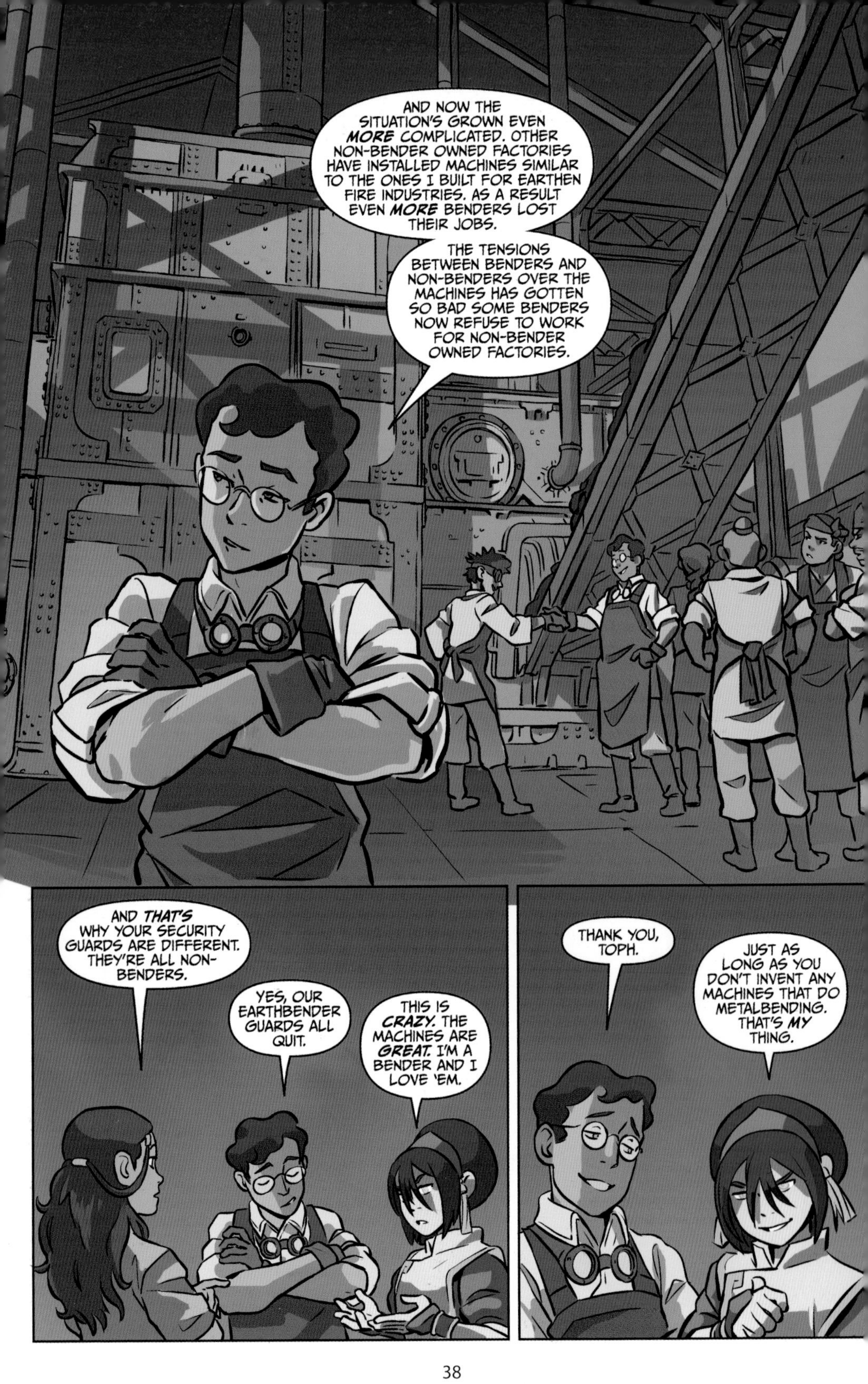
AND NOW THE SITUATION'S GROWN EVEN MORE COMPLICATED. OTHER NON-BENDER OWNED FACTORIES HAVE INSTALLED MACHINES SIMILAR TO THE ONES I BUILT FOR EARTHEN FIRE INDUSTRIES. AS A RESULT EVEN MORE BENDERS LOST THEIR JOBS.
THE TENSIONS BETWEEN BENDERS AND NON-BENDERS OVER THE MACHINES HAS GOTTEN SO BAD SOME BENDERS NOW REFUSE TO WORK FOR NON-BENDER OWNED FACTORIES.
AND THAT'S WHY YOUR SECURITY GUARDS ARE DIFFERENT. THEY'RE ALL NON-BENDERS.
YES, OUR EARTHBENDER GUARDS ALL QUIT.
THIS IS CRAZY. THE MACHINES ARE GREAT. I'M A BENDER AND I LOVE 'EM.
THANK YOU, TOPH.
JUST AS LONG AS YOU DON'T INVENT ANY MACHINES THAT DO METALBENDING. THAT'S MY THING.

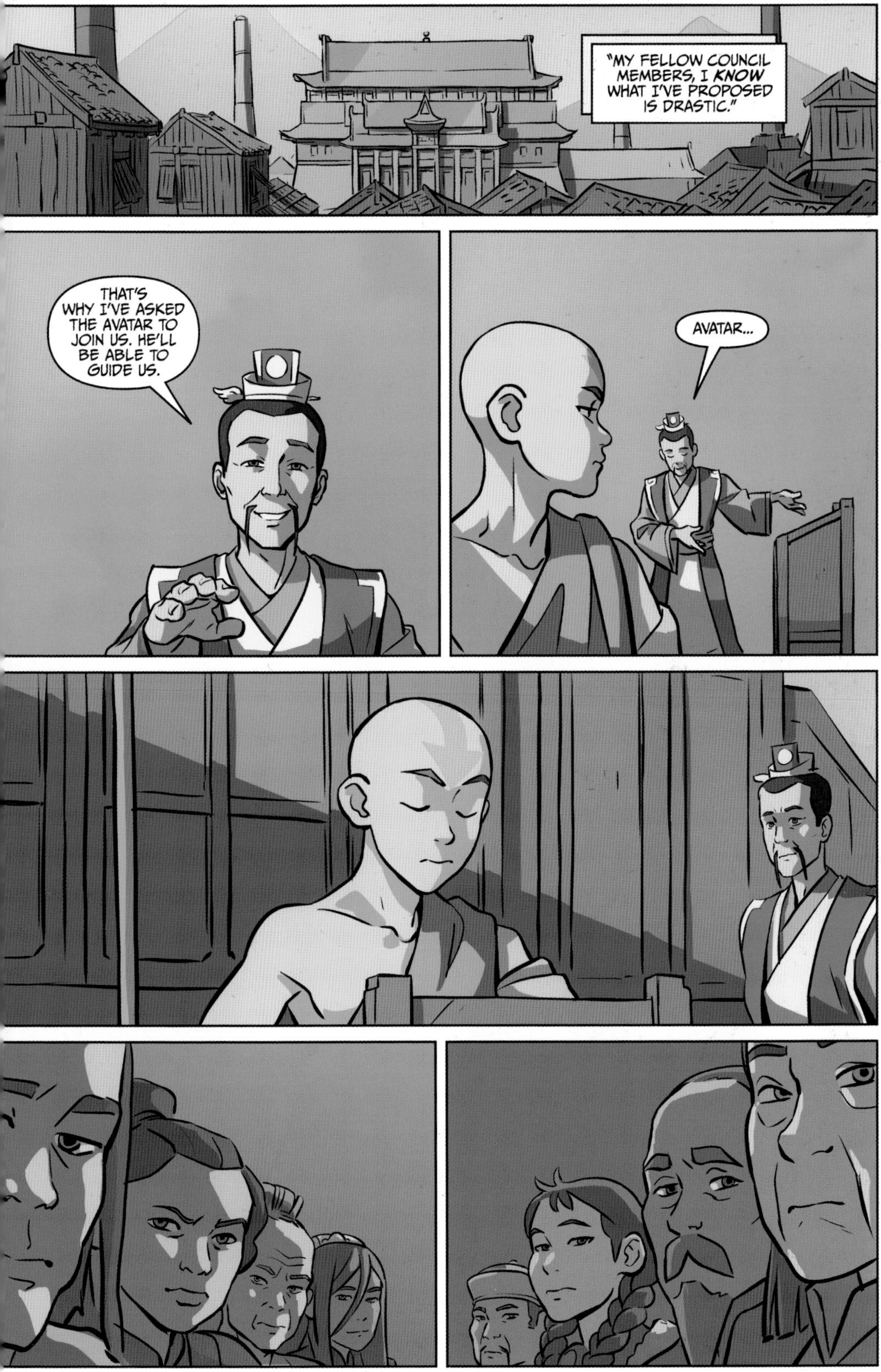
"MY FELLOW COUNCIL MEMBERS, I KNOW WHAT I'VE PROPOSED IS DRASTIC."
THAT'S WHY I'VE ASKED THE AVATAR TO JOIN US. HE'LL BE ABLE TO GUIDE US.
AVATAR...

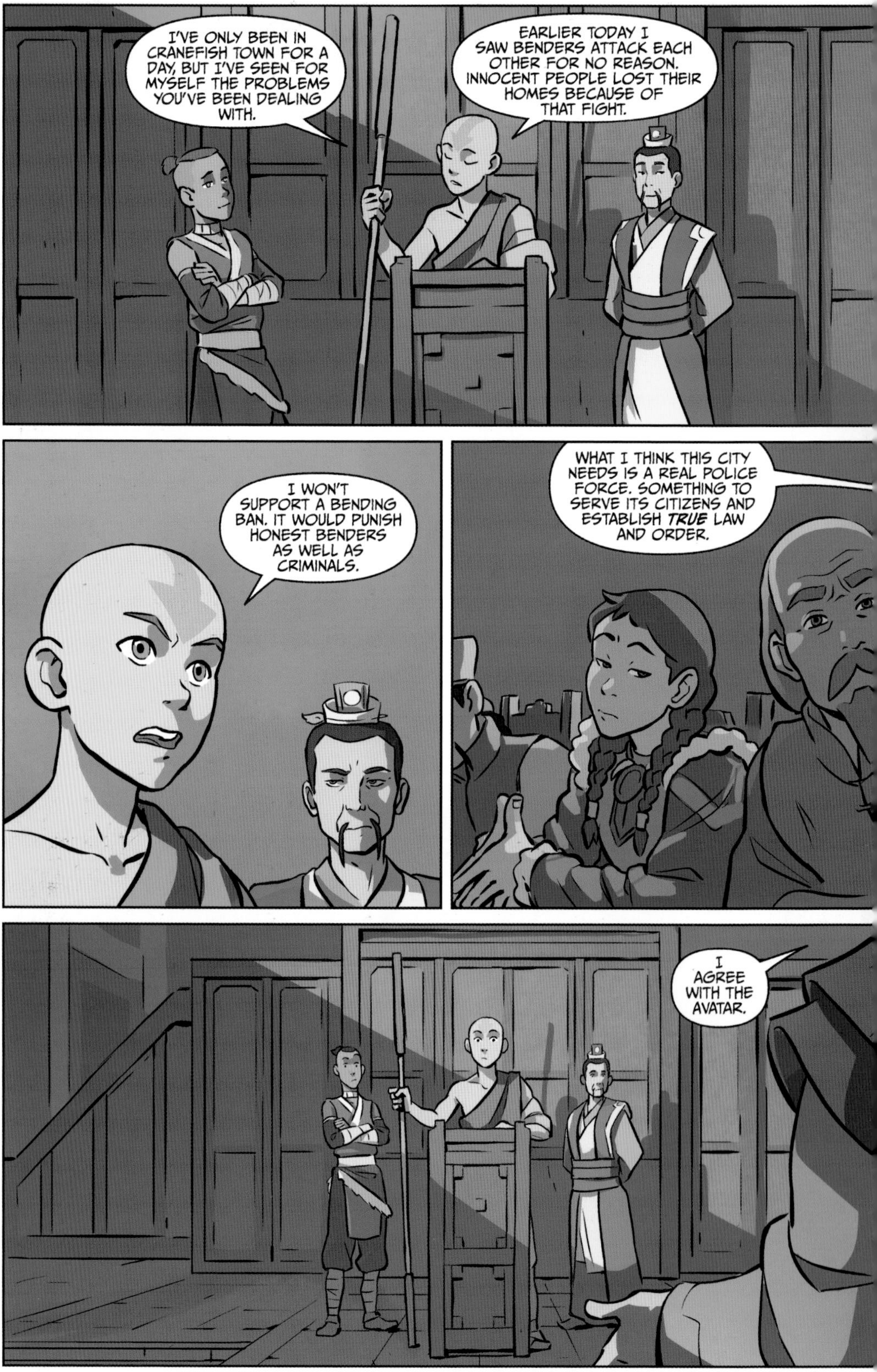
I'VE ONLY BEEN IN CRANEFISH TOWN FOR A DAY, BUT I'VE SEEN FOR MYSELF THE PROBLEMS YOU'VE BEEN DEALING WITH.
EARLIER TODAY I SAW BENDERS ATTACK EACH OTHER FOR NO REASON. INNOCENT PEOPLE LOST THEIR HOMES BECAUSE OF THAT FIGHT.
I WON'T SUPPORT A BENDING BAN. IT WOULD PUNISH HONEST BENDERS AS WELL AS CRIMINALS.
WHAT I THINK THIS CITY NEEDS IS A REAL POLICE FORCE. SOMETHING TO SERVE ITS CITIZENS AND ESTABLISH *TRUE* LAW AND ORDER.
I AGREE WITH THE AVATAR.

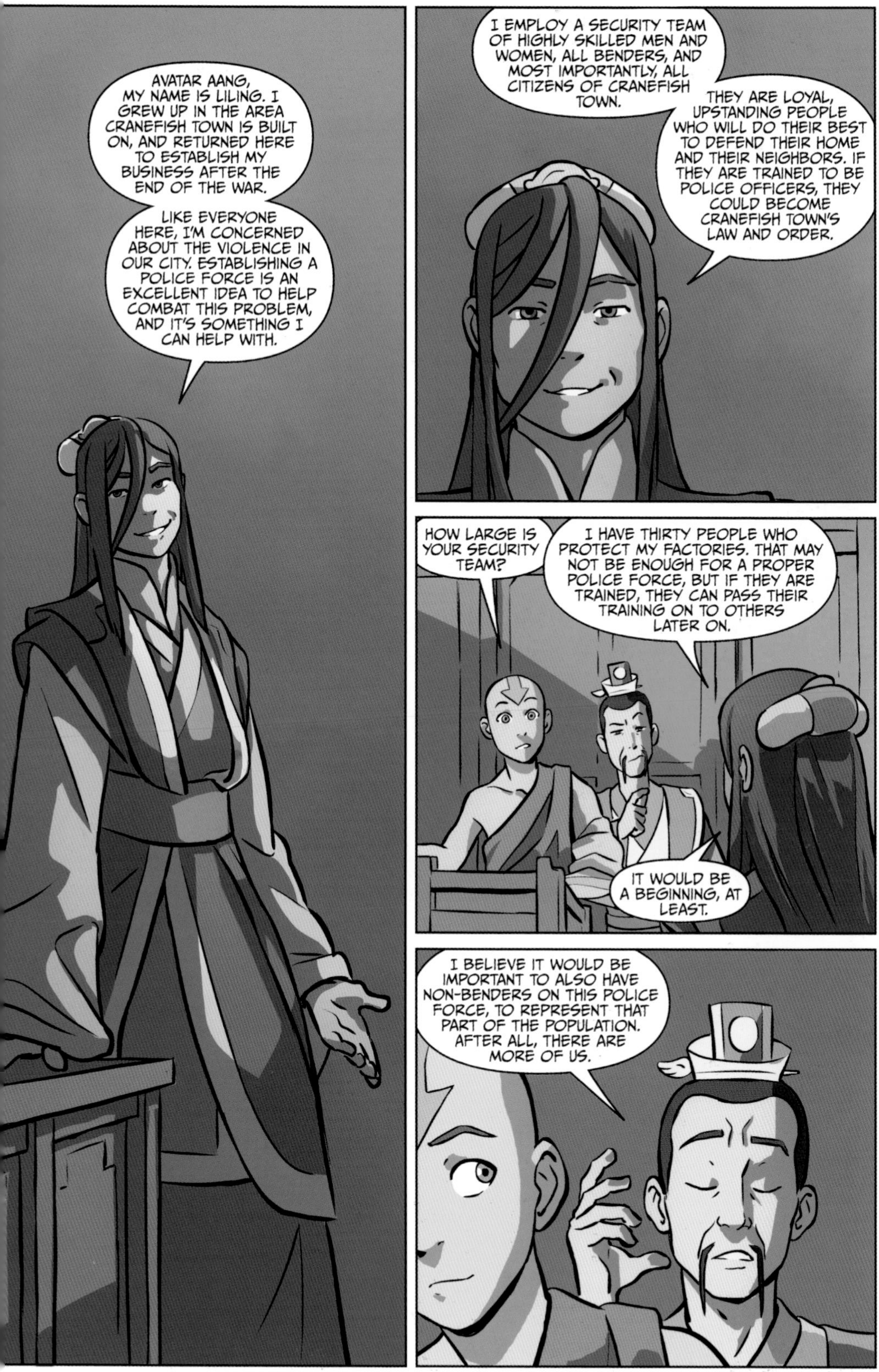
AVATAR AANG, MY NAME IS LILING. I GREW UP IN THE AREA CRANEFISH TOWN IS BUILT ON, AND RETURNED HERE TO ESTABLISH MY BUSINESS AFTER THE END OF THE WAR.
LIKE EVERYONE HERE, I'M CONCERNED ABOUT THE VIOLENCE IN OUR CITY. ESTABLISHING A POLICE FORCE IS AN EXCELLENT IDEA TO HELP COMBAT THIS PROBLEM, AND IT'S SOMETHING I CAN HELP WITH.
I EMPLOY A SECURITY TEAM OF HIGHLY SKILLED MEN AND WOMEN, ALL BENDERS, AND MOST IMPORTANTLY, ALL CITIZENS OF CRANEFISH TOWN.
THEY ARE LOYAL, UPSTANDING PEOPLE WHO WILL DO THEIR BEST TO DEFEND THEIR HOME AND THEIR NEIGHBORS. IF THEY ARE TRAINED TO BE POLICE OFFICERS, THEY COULD BECOME CRANEFISH TOWN'S LAW AND ORDER.
HOW LARGE IS YOUR SECURITY TEAM?
I HAVE THIRTY PEOPLE WHO PROTECT MY FACTORIES. THAT MAY NOT BE ENOUGH FOR A PROPER POLICE FORCE, BUT IF THEY ARE TRAINED, THEY CAN PASS THEIR TRAINING ON TO OTHERS LATER ON.
IT WOULD BE A BEGINNING, AT LEAST.
I BELIEVE IT WOULD BE IMPORTANT TO ALSO HAVE NON-BENDERS ON THIS POLICE FORCE, TO REPRESENT THAT PART OF THE POPULATION. AFTER ALL, THERE ARE MORE OF US.

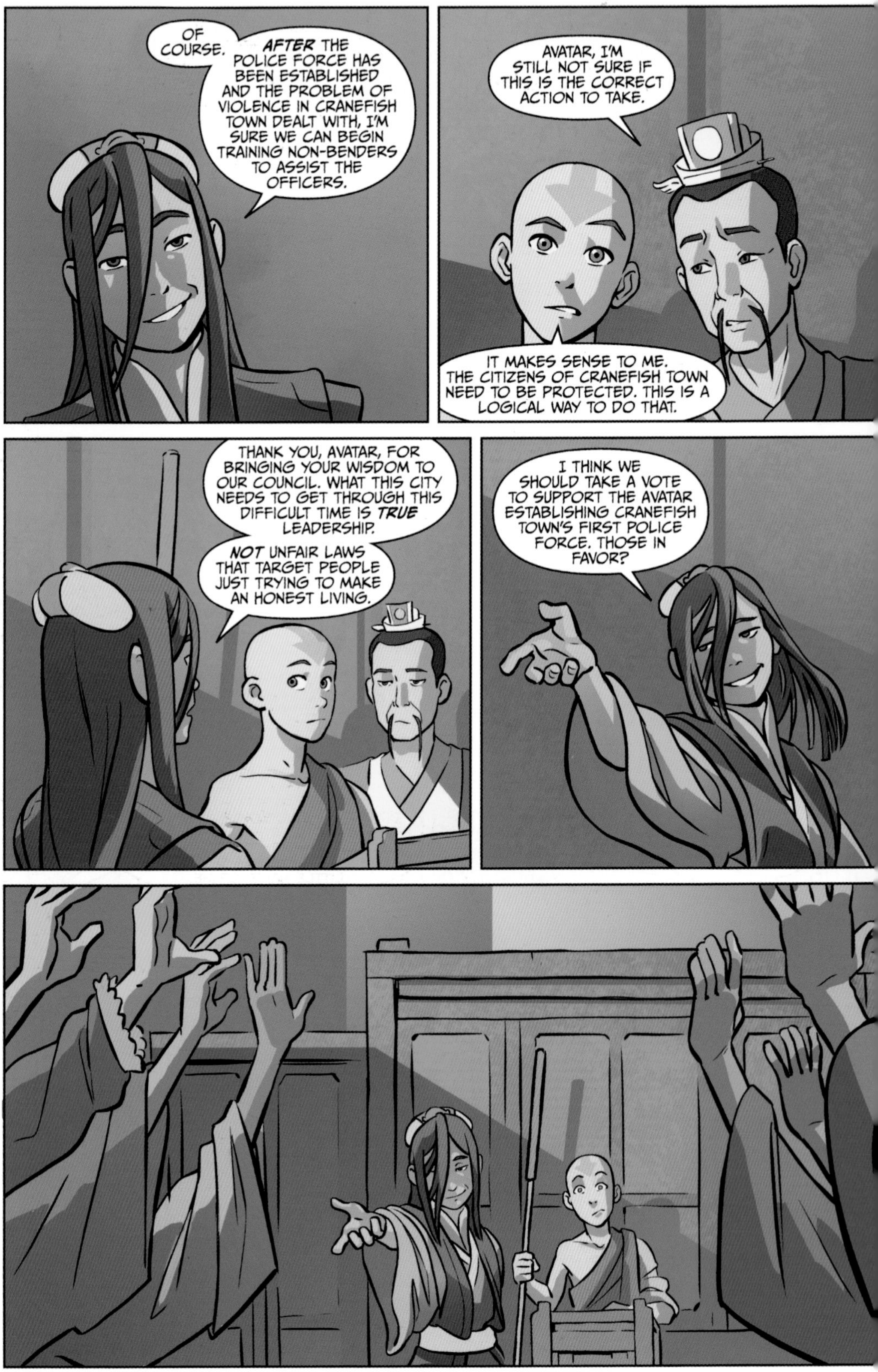
OF COURSE.
AFTER THE POLICE FORCE HAS BEEN ESTABLISHED AND THE PROBLEM OF VIOLENCE IN CRANEFISH TOWN DEALT WITH, I'M SURE WE CAN BEGIN TRAINING NON-BENDERS TO ASSIST THE OFFICERS.
AVATAR, I'M STILL NOT SURE IF THIS IS THE CORRECT ACTION TO TAKE.
IT MAKES SENSE TO ME. THE CITIZENS OF CRANEFISH TOWN NEED TO BE PROTECTED. THIS IS A LOGICAL WAY TO DO THAT.
THANK YOU, AVATAR, FOR BRINGING YOUR WISDOM TO OUR COUNCIL. WHAT THIS CITY NEEDS TO GET THROUGH THIS DIFFICULT TIME IS *TRUE* LEADERSHIP.
NOT UNFAIR LAWS THAT TARGET PEOPLE JUST TRYING TO MAKE AN HONEST LIVING.
I THINK WE SHOULD TAKE A VOTE TO SUPPORT THE AVATAR ESTABLISHING CRANEFISH TOWN'S FIRST POLICE FORCE. THOSE IN FAVOR?

WE *BELIEVE* IN YOU, AVATAR.

THAT COUNCIL LADY SEEMED ALL RIGHT, VOLUNTEERING HER OWN SECURITY TEAM TO HELP CLEAN UP CRANEFISH TOWN'S STREETS.

YES, EVERYONE WANTED TO HELP.

WE'RE DEFINITELY SPENDING LONGER THAN JUST A DAY HERE, HUH?

LOOKS LIKE. I DON'T THINK WE'LL BE GETTING TO YU DAO ANYTIME SOON.

IN THAT CASE, I'M GONNA SEND A MESSENGER HAWK TO SUKI AND TELL HER TO JOIN US HERE.

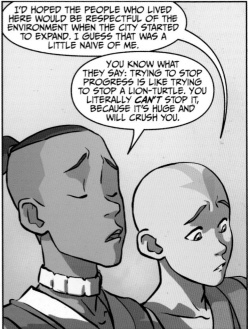

I'D HOPED THE PEOPLE WHO LIVED HERE WOULD BE RESPECTFUL OF THE ENVIRONMENT WHEN THE CITY STARTED TO EXPAND. I GUESS THAT WAS A LITTLE NAIVE OF ME.

YOU KNOW WHAT THEY SAY: TRYING TO STOP PROGRESS IS LIKE TRYING TO STOP A LION-TURTLE. YOU LITERALLY *CAN'T* STOP IT, BECAUSE IT'S HUGE AND WILL CRUSH YOU.

43

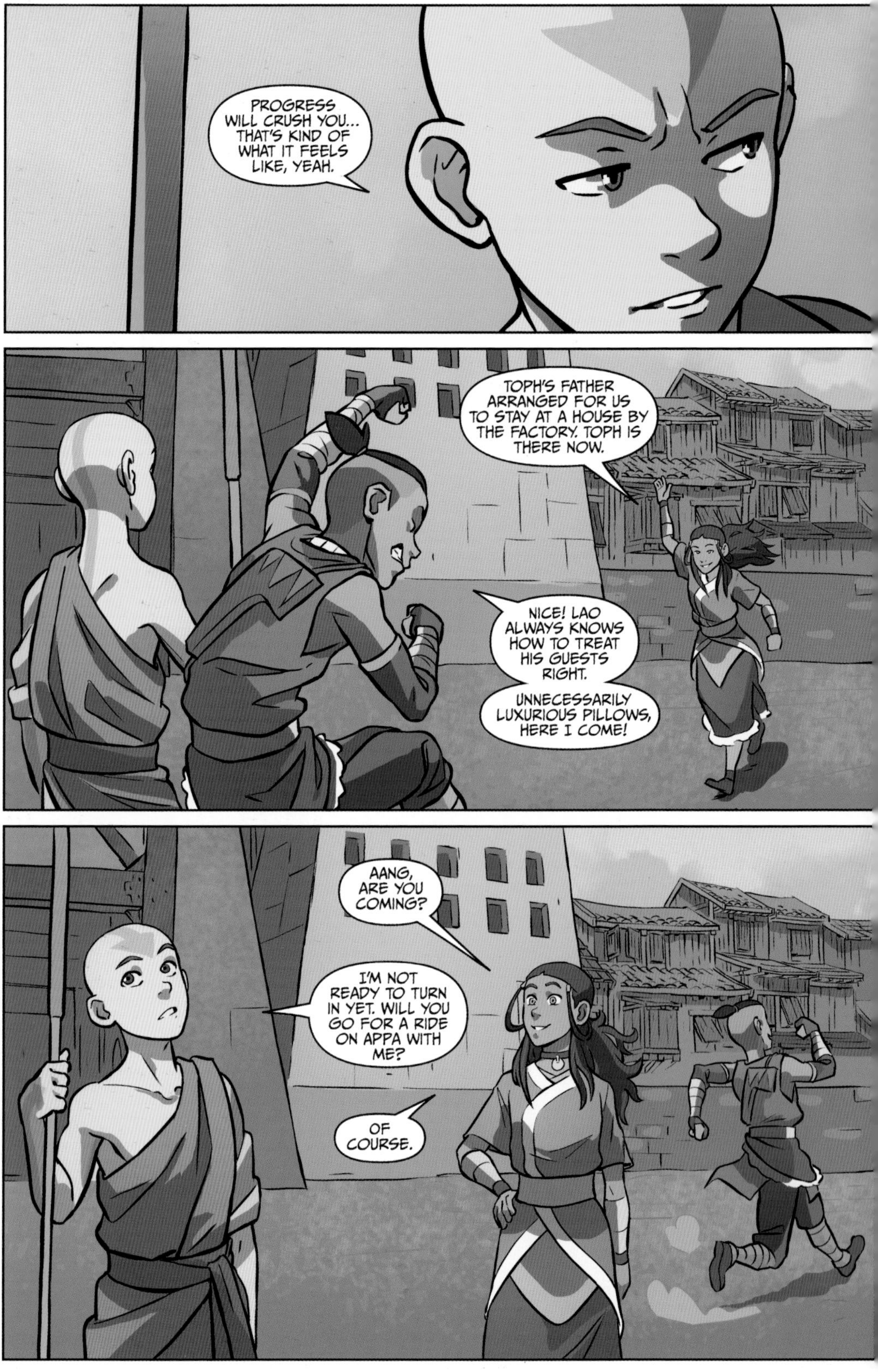
PROGRESS WILL CRUSH YOU... THAT'S KIND OF WHAT IT FEELS LIKE, YEAH.
TOPH'S FATHER ARRANGED FOR US TO STAY AT A HOUSE BY THE FACTORY. TOPH IS THERE NOW.
NICE! LAO ALWAYS KNOWS HOW TO TREAT HIS GUESTS RIGHT.
UNNECESSARILY LUXURIOUS PILLOWS, HERE I COME!
AANG, ARE YOU COMING?
I'M NOT READY TO TURN IN YET. WILL YOU GO FOR A RIDE ON APPA WITH ME?
OF COURSE.

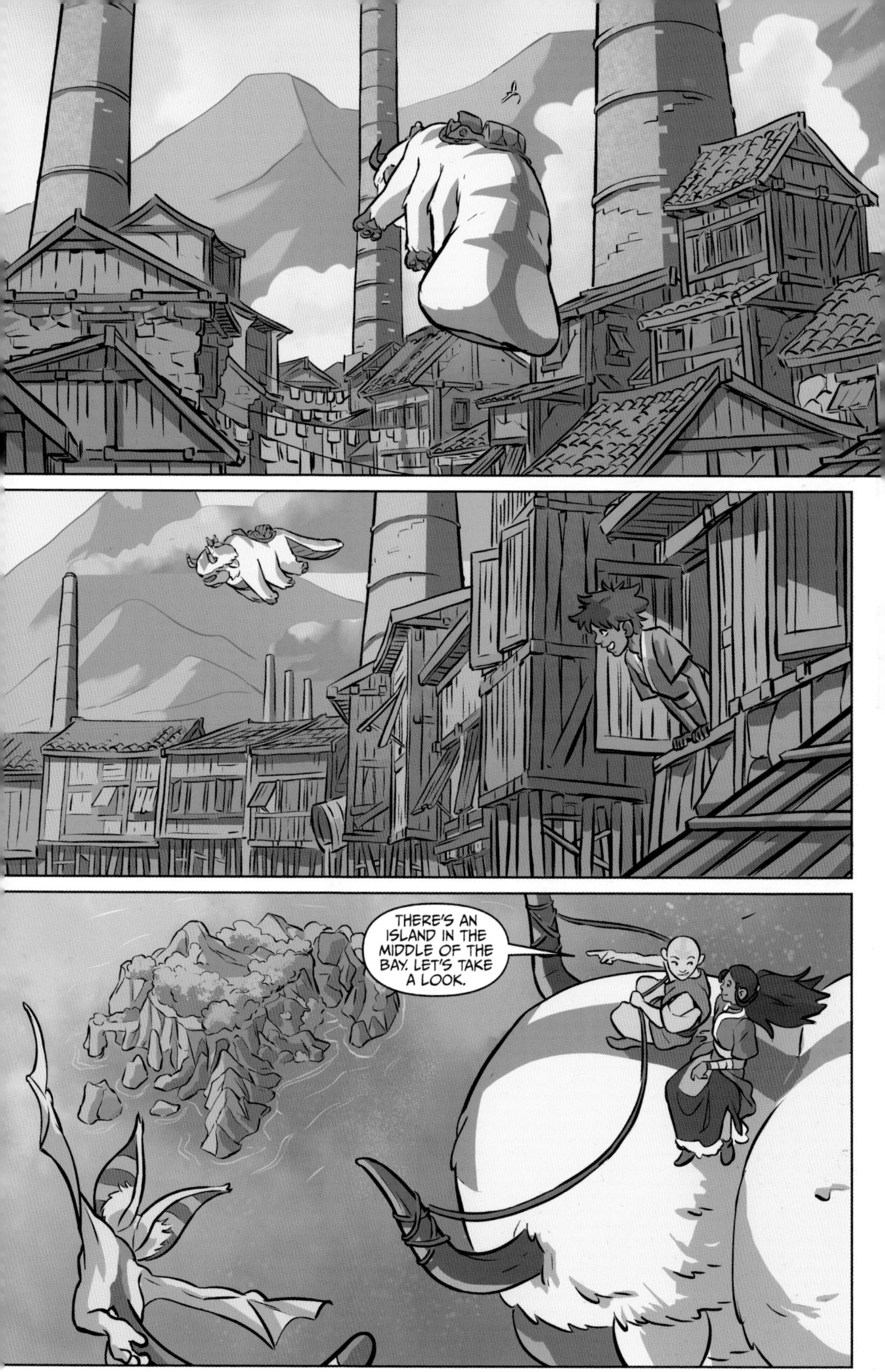
THERE'S AN ISLAND IN THE MIDDLE OF THE BAY. LET'S TAKE A LOOK.

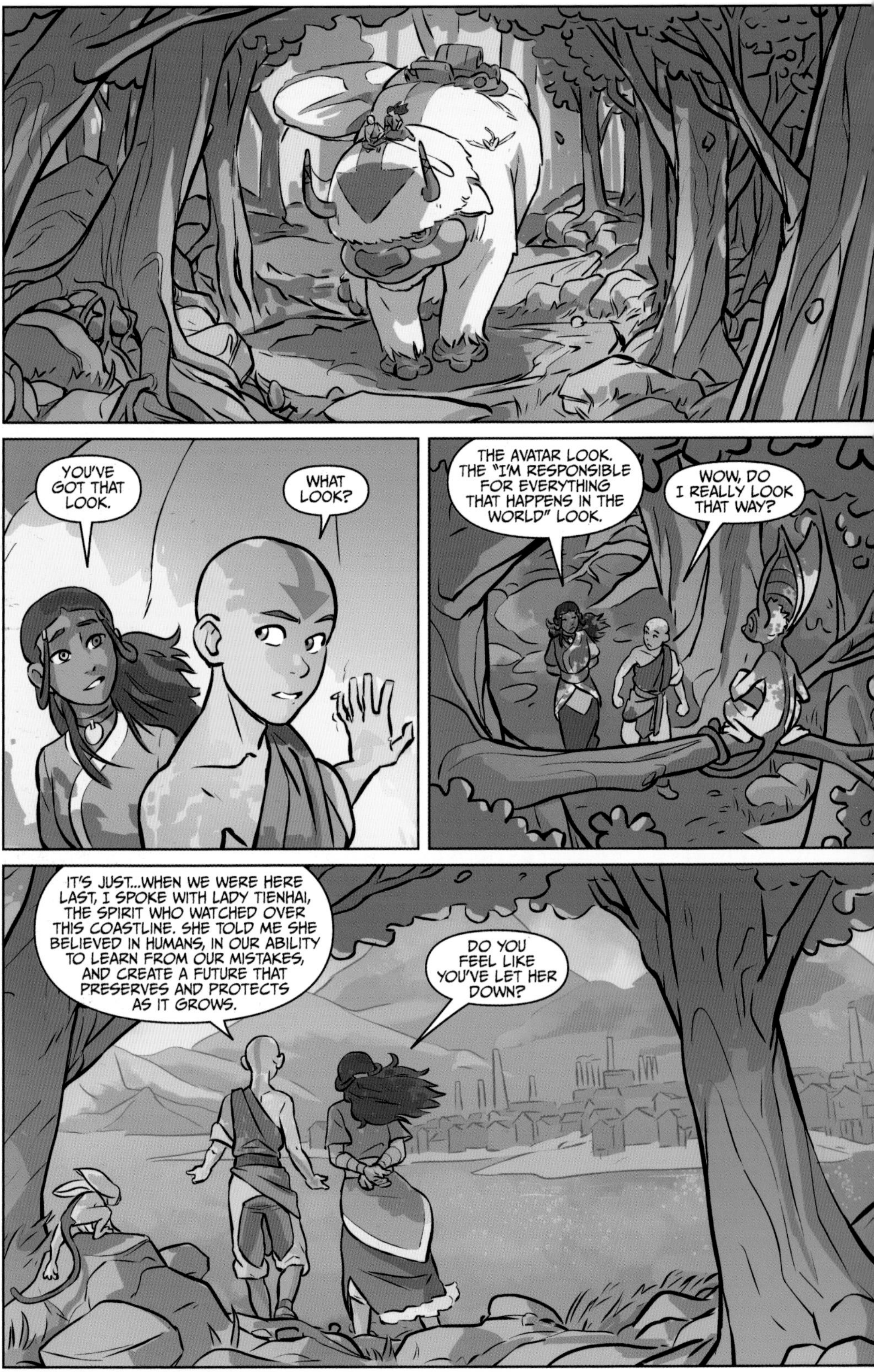
YOU'VE GOT THAT LOOK.
WHAT LOOK?
THE AVATAR LOOK. THE "I'M RESPONSIBLE FOR EVERYTHING THAT HAPPENS IN THE WORLD" LOOK.
WOW, DO I REALLY LOOK THAT WAY?
IT'S JUST...WHEN WE WERE HERE LAST, I SPOKE WITH LADY TIENHAI, THE SPIRIT WHO WATCHED OVER THIS COASTLINE. SHE TOLD ME SHE BELIEVED IN HUMANS, IN OUR ABILITY TO LEARN FROM OUR MISTAKES, AND CREATE A FUTURE THAT PRESERVES AND PROTECTS AS IT GROWS.
DO YOU FEEL LIKE YOU'VE LET HER DOWN?

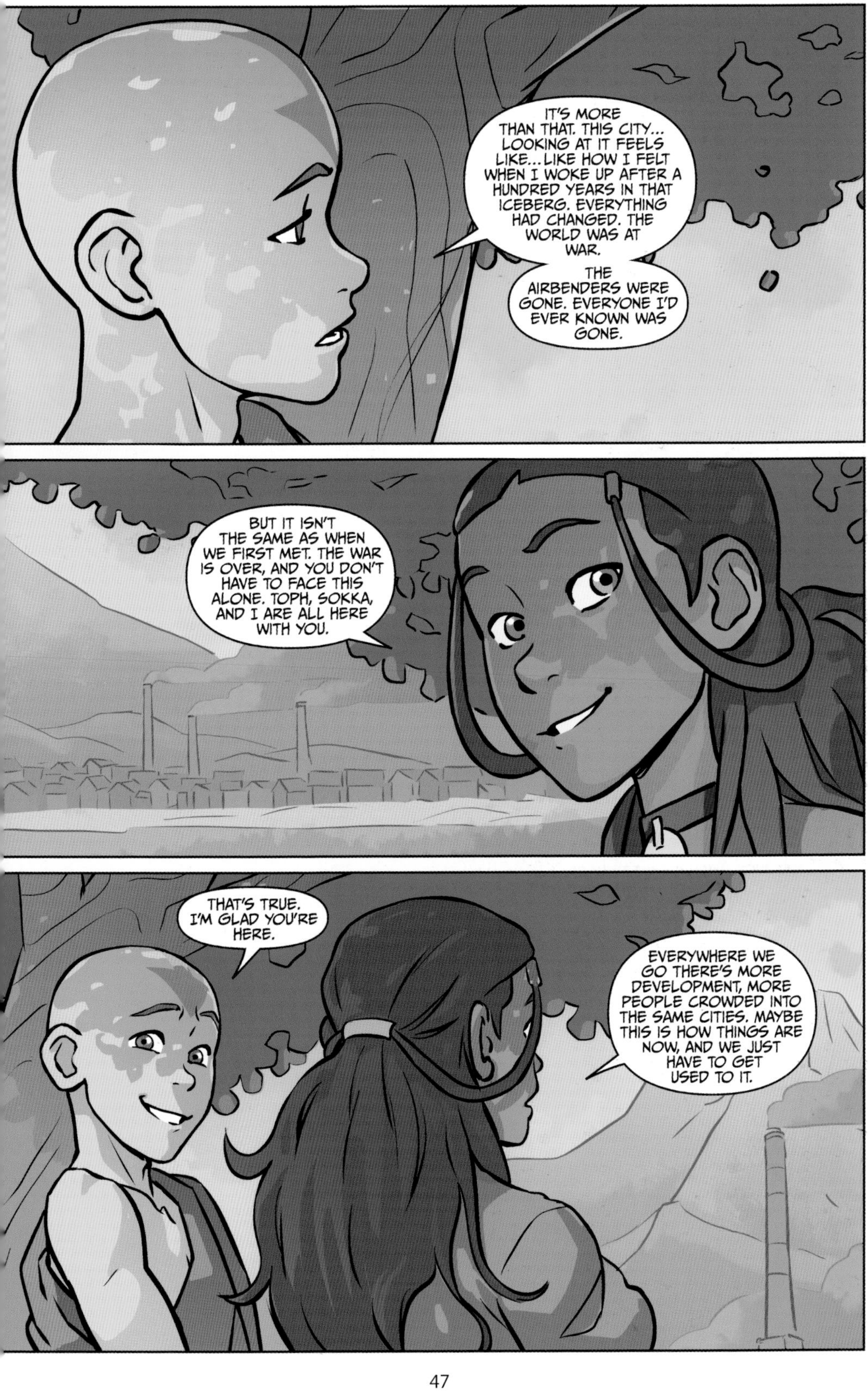
IT'S MORE THAN THAT. THIS CITY... LOOKING AT IT FEELS LIKE...LIKE HOW I FELT WHEN I WOKE UP AFTER A HUNDRED YEARS IN THAT ICEBERG. EVERYTHING HAD CHANGED. THE WORLD WAS AT WAR.
THE AIRBENDERS WERE GONE. EVERYONE I'D EVER KNOWN WAS GONE.
BUT IT ISN'T THE SAME AS WHEN WE FIRST MET. THE WAR IS OVER, AND YOU DON'T HAVE TO FACE THIS ALONE. TOPH, SOKKA, AND I ARE ALL HERE WITH YOU.
THAT'S TRUE. I'M GLAD YOU'RE HERE.
EVERYWHERE WE GO THERE'S MORE DEVELOPMENT, MORE PEOPLE CROWDED INTO THE SAME CITIES. MAYBE THIS IS HOW THINGS ARE NOW, AND WE JUST HAVE TO GET USED TO IT.

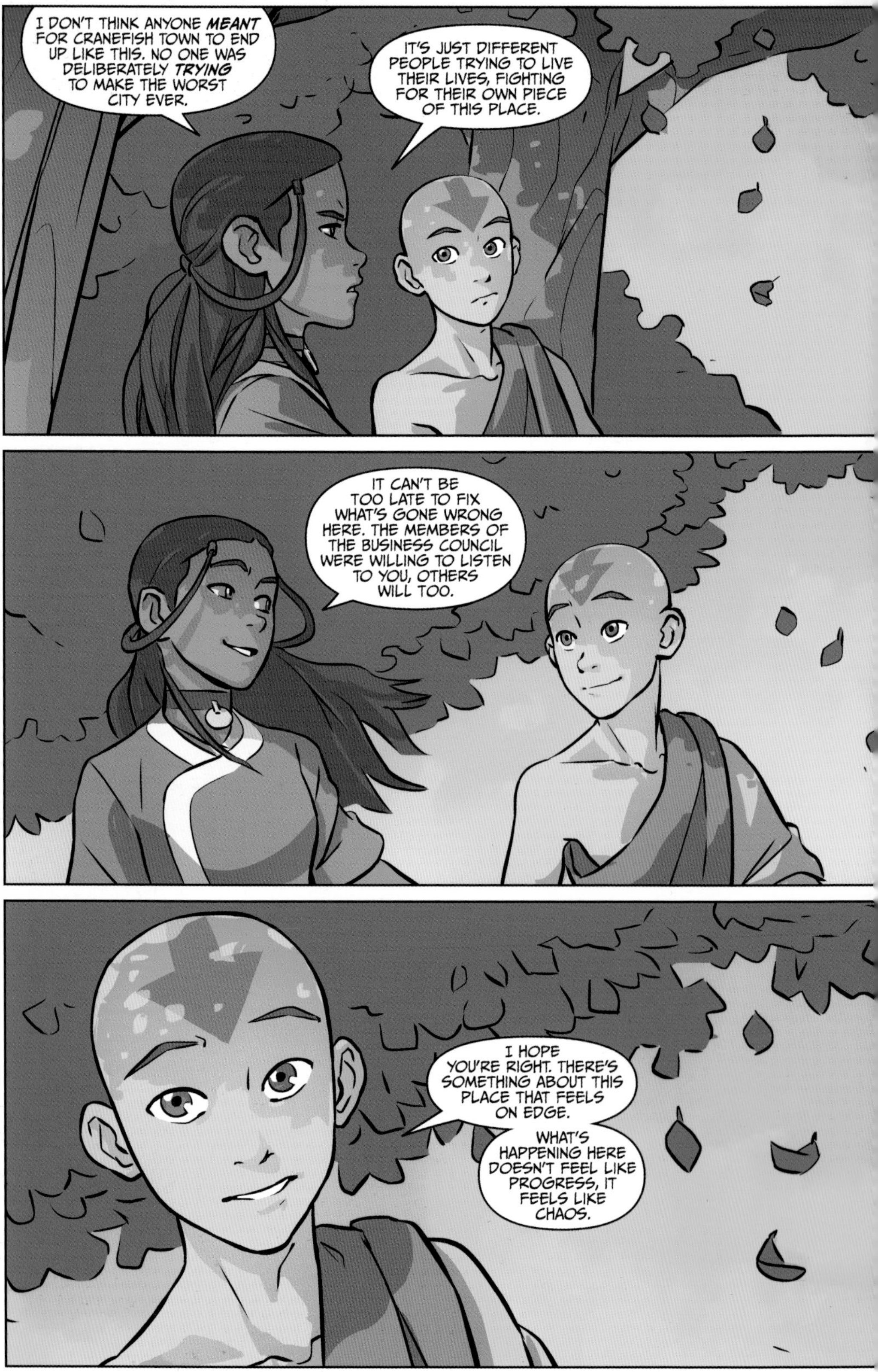
I DON'T THINK ANYONE *MEANT* FOR CRANEFISH TOWN TO END UP LIKE THIS. NO ONE WAS DELIBERATELY *TRYING* TO MAKE THE WORST CITY EVER.
IT'S JUST DIFFERENT PEOPLE TRYING TO LIVE THEIR LIVES, FIGHTING FOR THEIR OWN PIECE OF THIS PLACE.
IT CAN'T BE TOO LATE TO FIX WHAT'S GONE WRONG HERE. THE MEMBERS OF THE BUSINESS COUNCIL WERE WILLING TO LISTEN TO YOU, OTHERS WILL TOO.
I HOPE YOU'RE RIGHT. THERE'S SOMETHING ABOUT THIS PLACE THAT FEELS ON EDGE.
WHAT'S HAPPENING HERE DOESN'T FEEL LIKE PROGRESS, IT FEELS LIKE CHAOS.

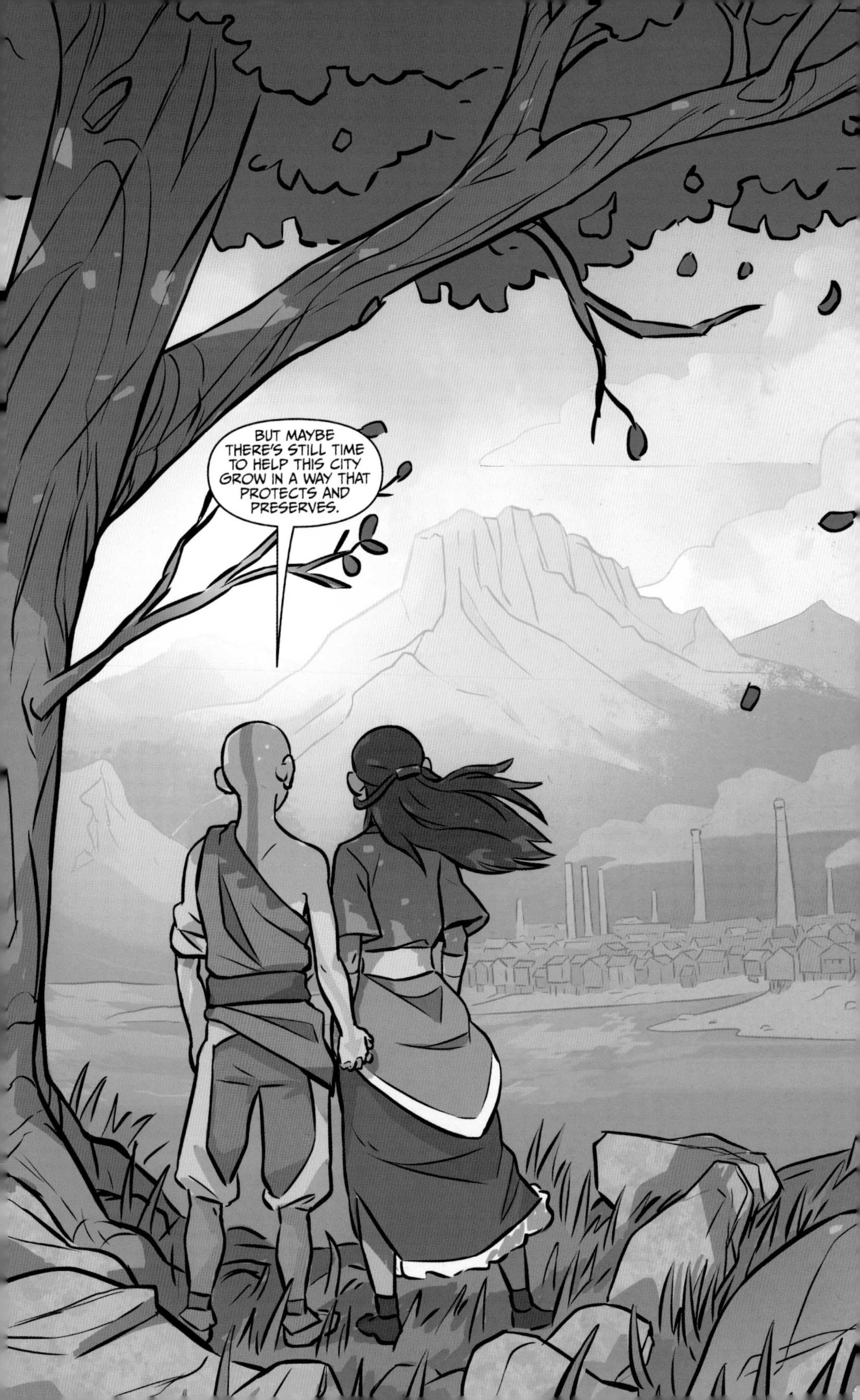
BUT MAYBE THERE'S STILL TIME TO HELP THIS CITY GROW IN A WAY THAT PROTECTS AND PRESERVES.

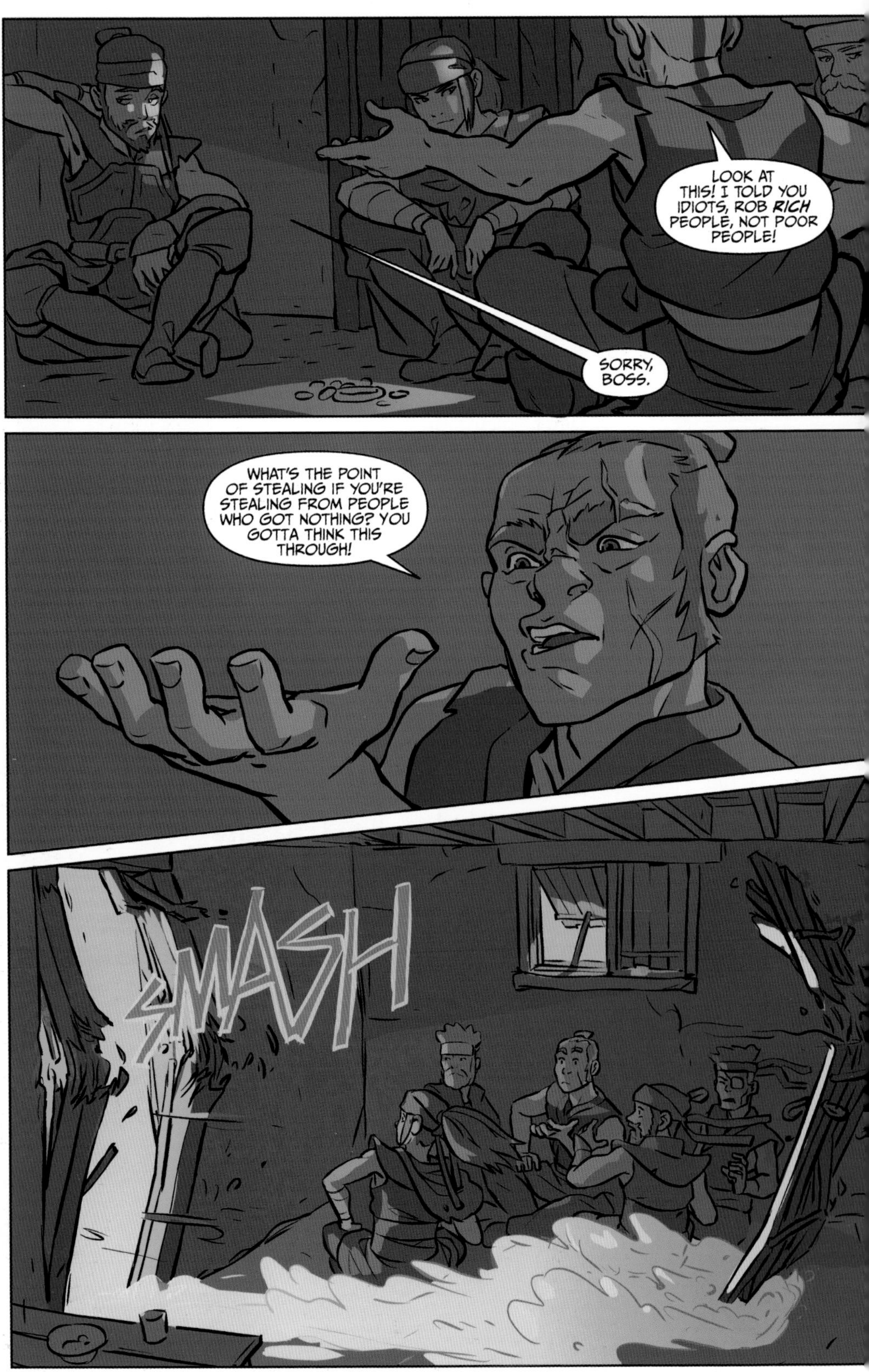
LOOK AT THIS! I TOLD YOU IDIOTS, ROB RICH PEOPLE, NOT POOR PEOPLE!
SORRY, BOSS.
WHAT'S THE POINT OF STEALING IF YOU'RE STEALING FROM PEOPLE WHO GOT NOTHING? YOU GOTTA THINK THIS THROUGH!
SMASH

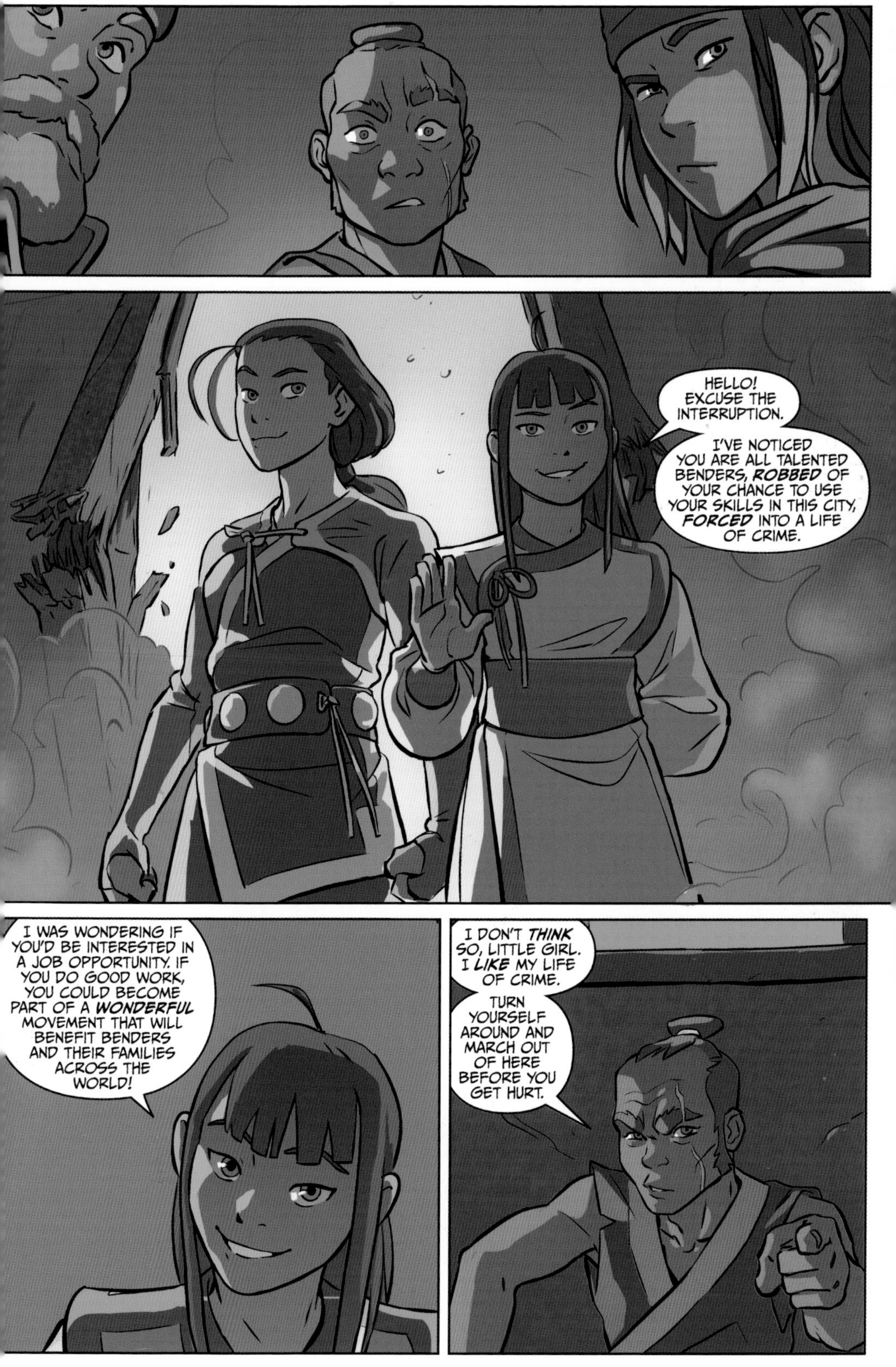
HELLO! EXCUSE THE INTERRUPTION.
I'VE NOTICED YOU ARE ALL TALENTED BENDERS, **ROBBED** OF YOUR CHANCE TO USE YOUR SKILLS IN THIS CITY, **FORCED** INTO A LIFE OF CRIME.
I WAS WONDERING IF YOU'D BE INTERESTED IN A JOB OPPORTUNITY. IF YOU DO GOOD WORK, YOU COULD BECOME PART OF A **WONDERFUL** MOVEMENT THAT WILL BENEFIT BENDERS AND THEIR FAMILIES ACROSS THE WORLD!
I DON'T **THINK** SO, LITTLE GIRL. I **LIKE** MY LIFE OF CRIME.
TURN YOURSELF AROUND AND MARCH OUT OF HERE BEFORE YOU GET HURT.

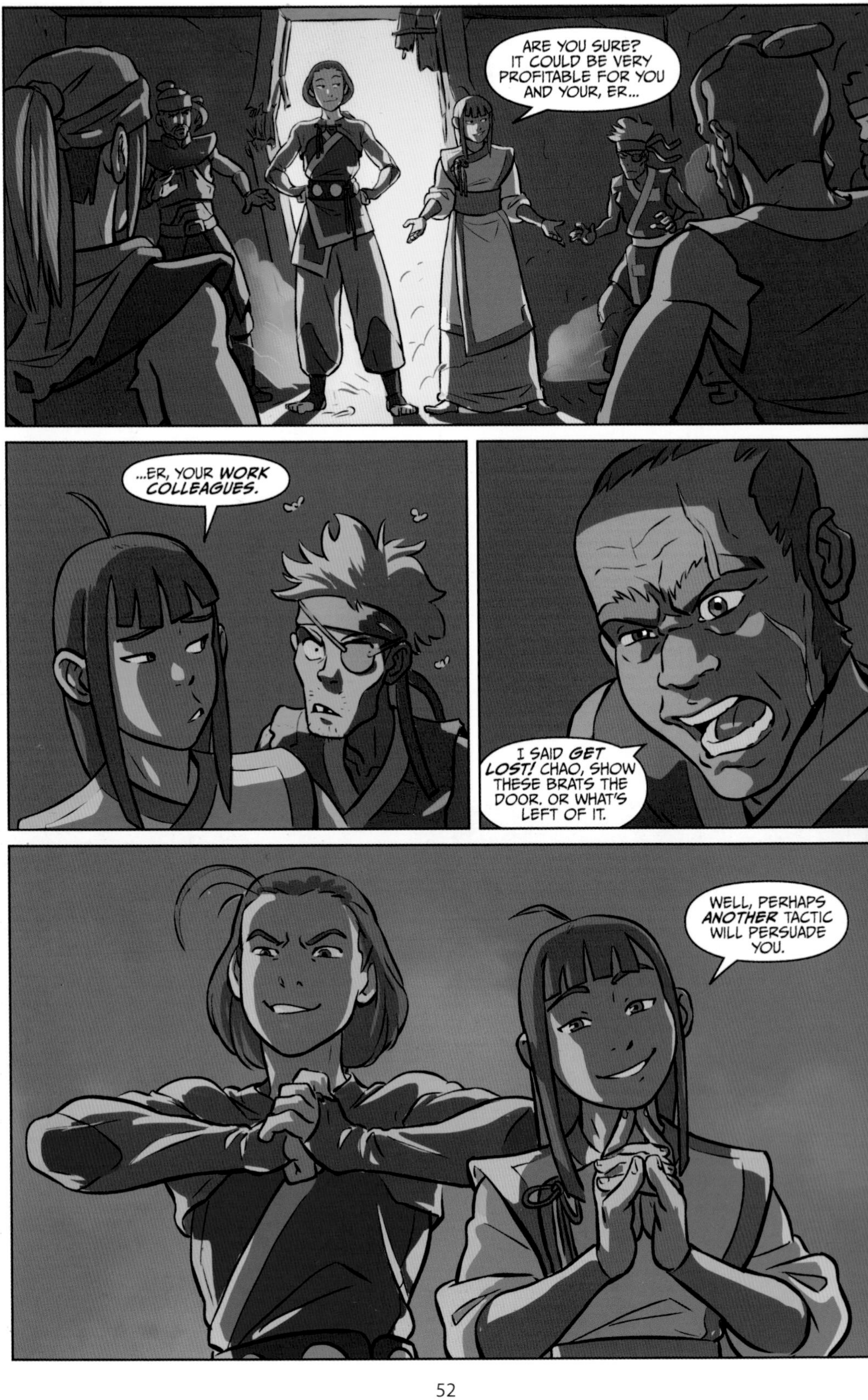
ARE YOU SURE? IT COULD BE VERY PROFITABLE FOR YOU AND YOUR, ER...
...ER, YOUR **WORK COLLEAGUES.**
I SAID ***GET LOST!*** CHAO, SHOW THESE BRATS THE DOOR. OR WHAT'S LEFT OF IT.
WELL, PERHAPS ***ANOTHER*** TACTIC WILL PERSUADE YOU.

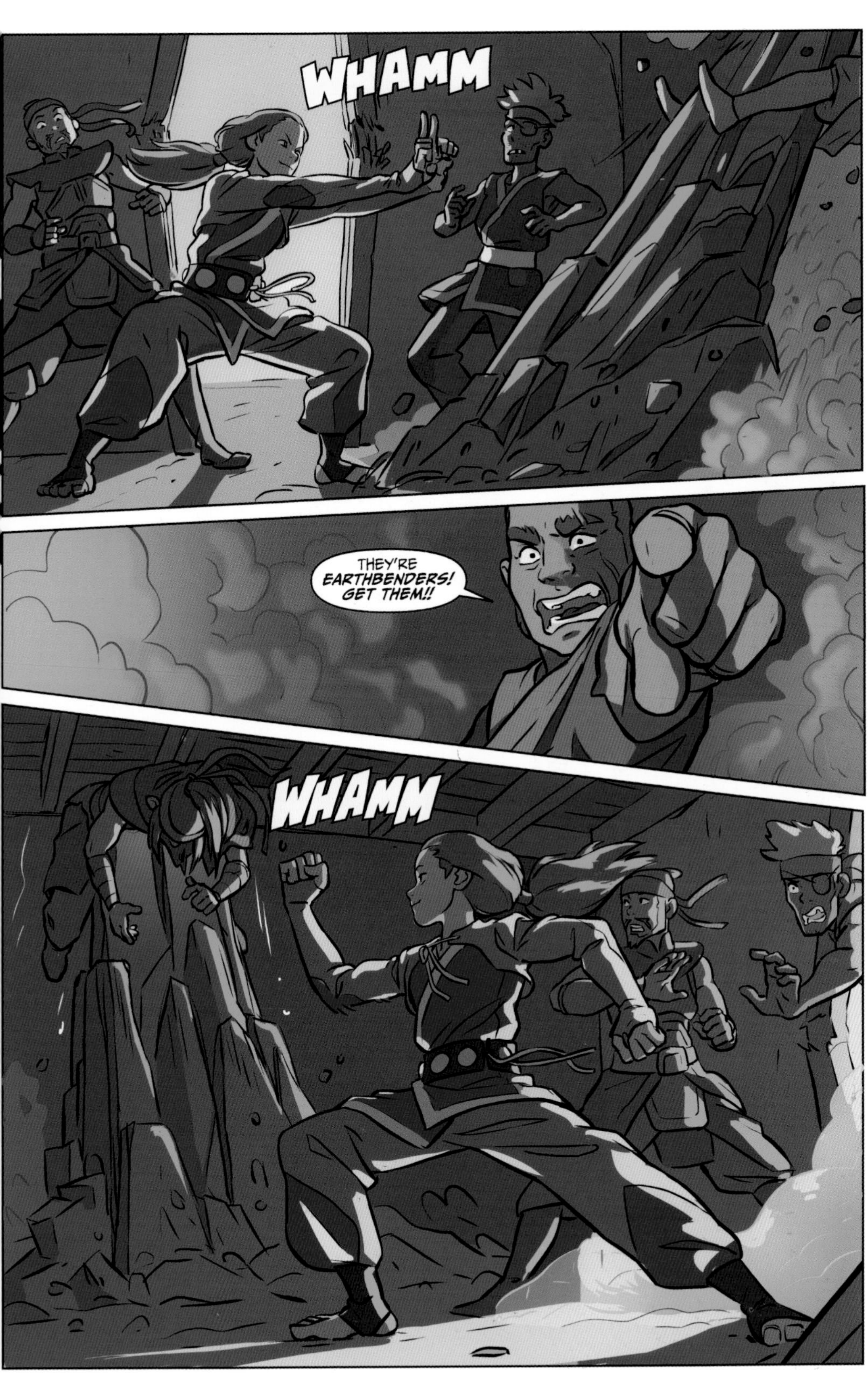
WHAMM
THEY'RE EARTHBENDERS! GET THEM!!
WHAMM

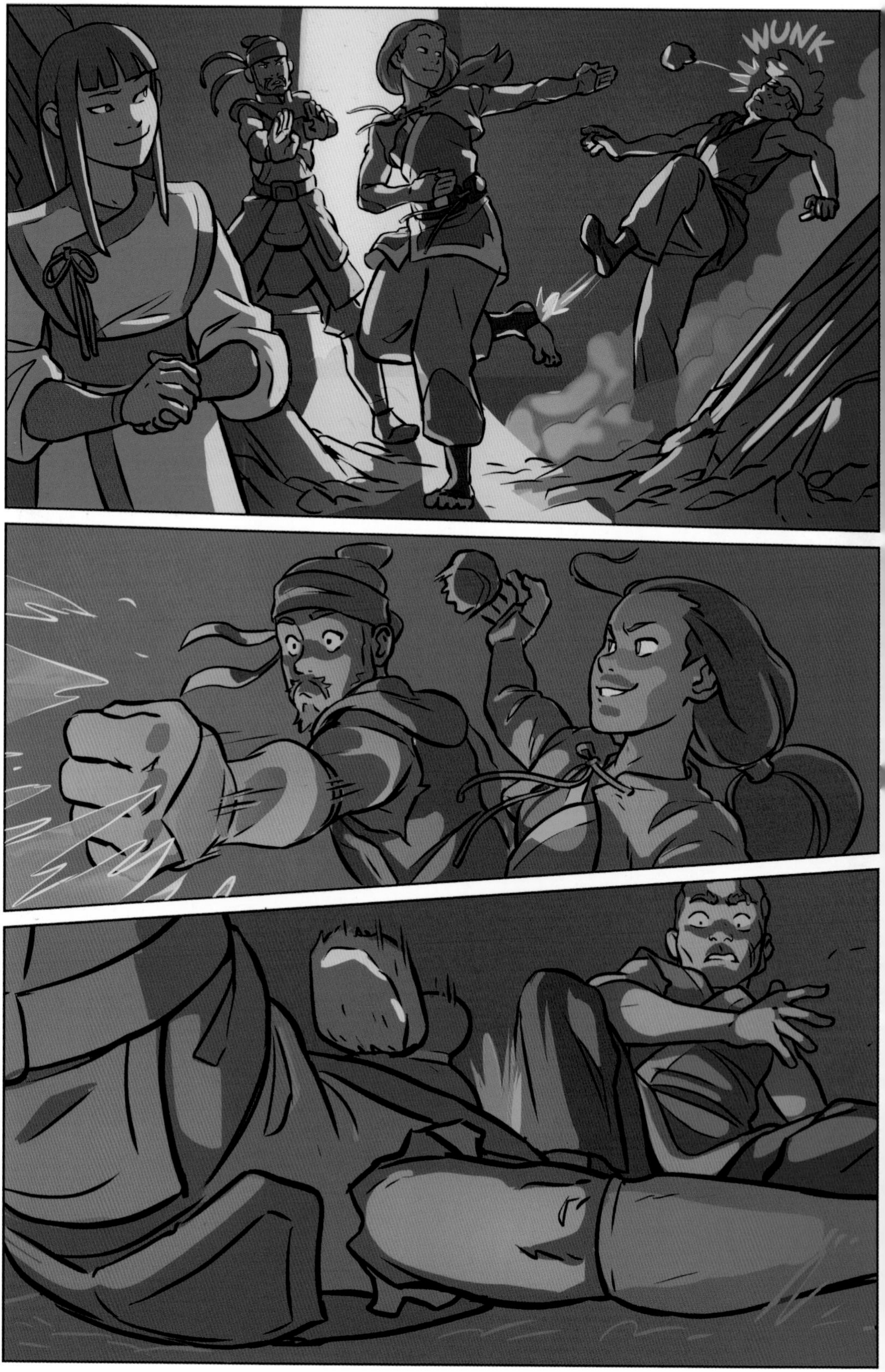
WUNK

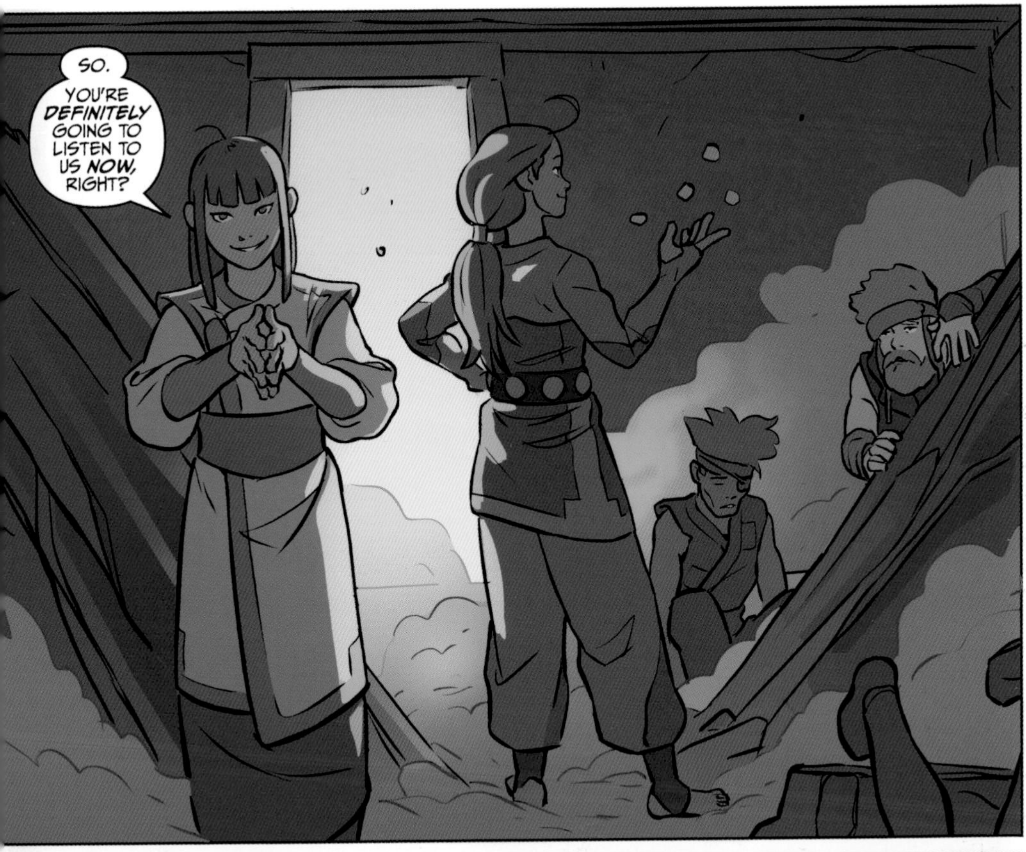
SO.
YOU'RE *DEFINITELY* GOING TO LISTEN TO US *NOW,* RIGHT?

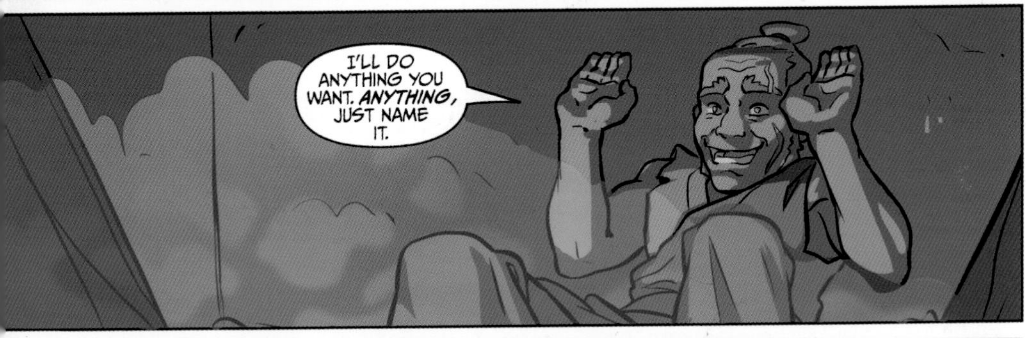
I'LL DO ANYTHING YOU WANT. *ANYTHING,* JUST NAME IT.

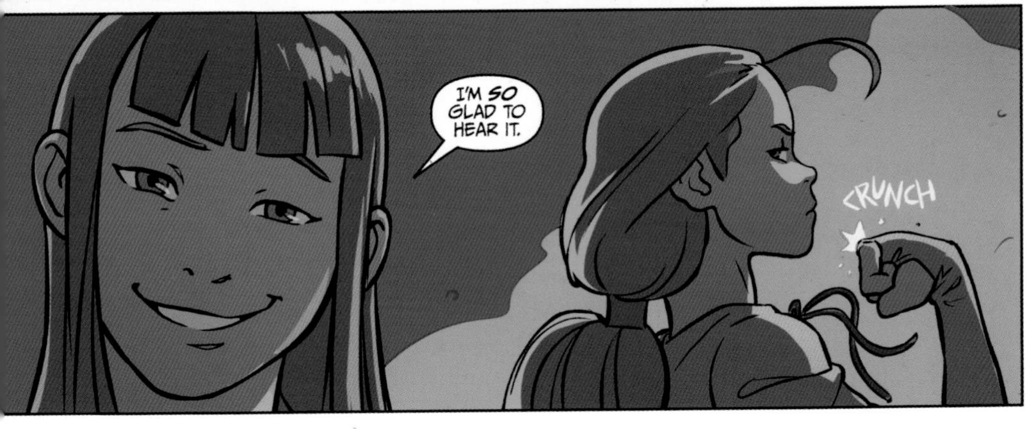
I'M *SO* GLAD TO HEAR IT.
CRUNCH

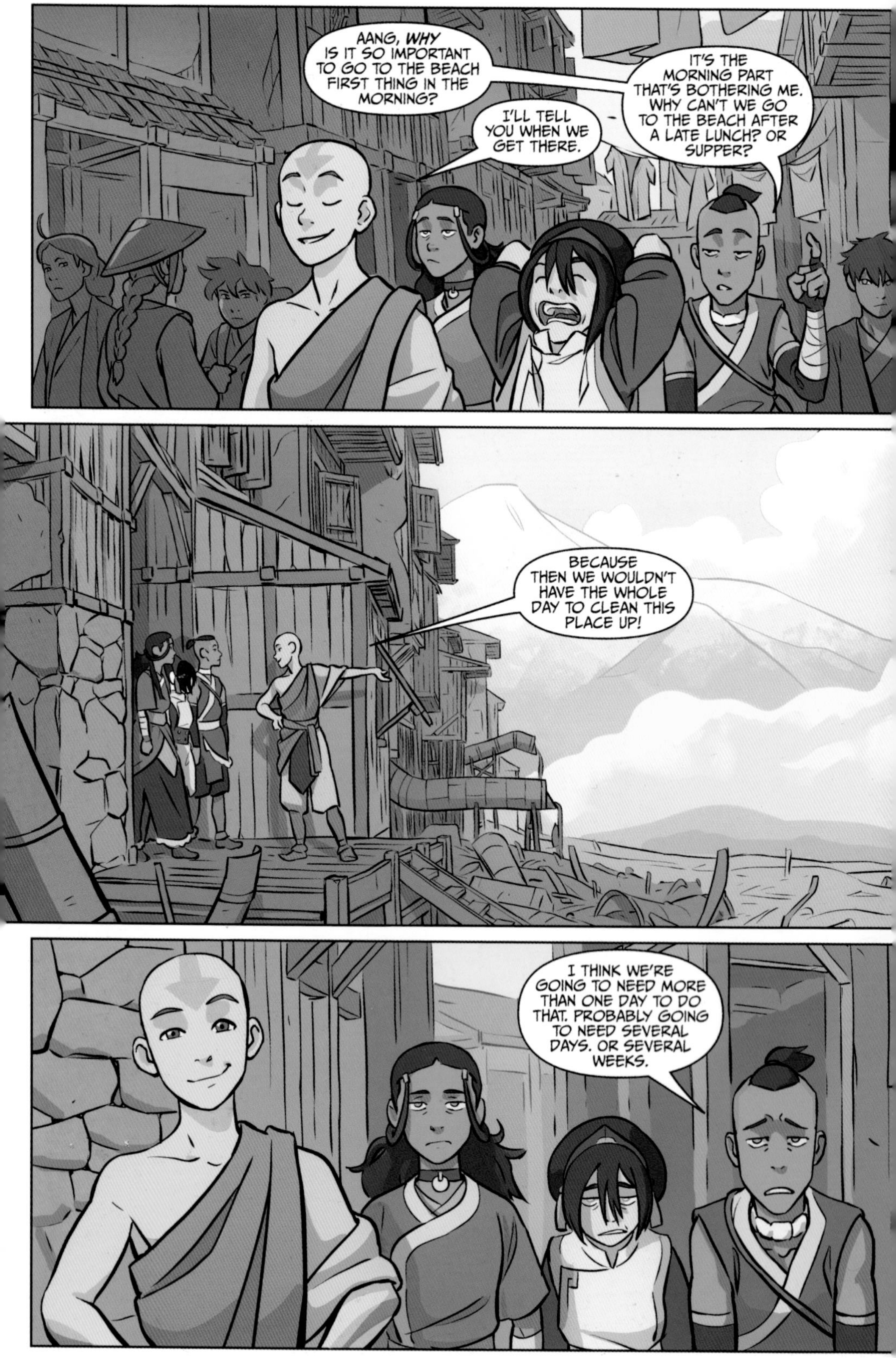
AANG, *WHY* IS IT SO IMPORTANT TO GO TO THE BEACH FIRST THING IN THE MORNING?
I'LL TELL YOU WHEN WE GET THERE.
IT'S THE MORNING PART THAT'S BOTHERING ME. WHY CAN'T WE GO TO THE BEACH AFTER A LATE LUNCH? OR SUPPER?
BECAUSE THEN WE WOULDN'T HAVE THE WHOLE DAY TO CLEAN THIS PLACE UP!
I THINK WE'RE GOING TO NEED MORE THAN ONE DAY TO DO THAT. PROBABLY GOING TO NEED SEVERAL DAYS. OR SEVERAL WEEKS.

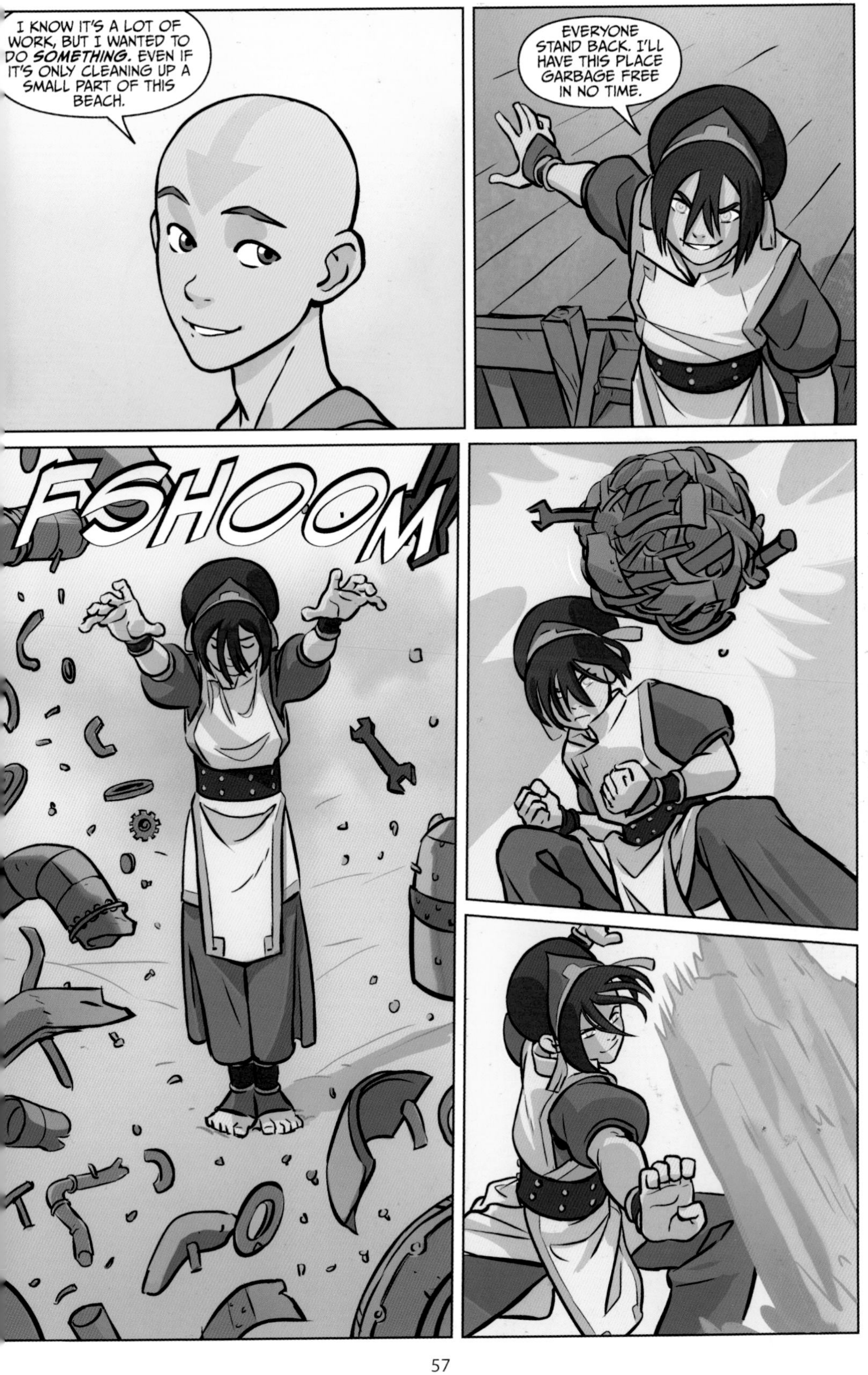
I KNOW IT'S A LOT OF WORK, BUT I WANTED TO DO **SOMETHING**. EVEN IF IT'S ONLY CLEANING UP A SMALL PART OF THIS BEACH.
EVERYONE STAND BACK. I'LL HAVE THIS PLACE GARBAGE FREE IN NO TIME.
FSHOOM

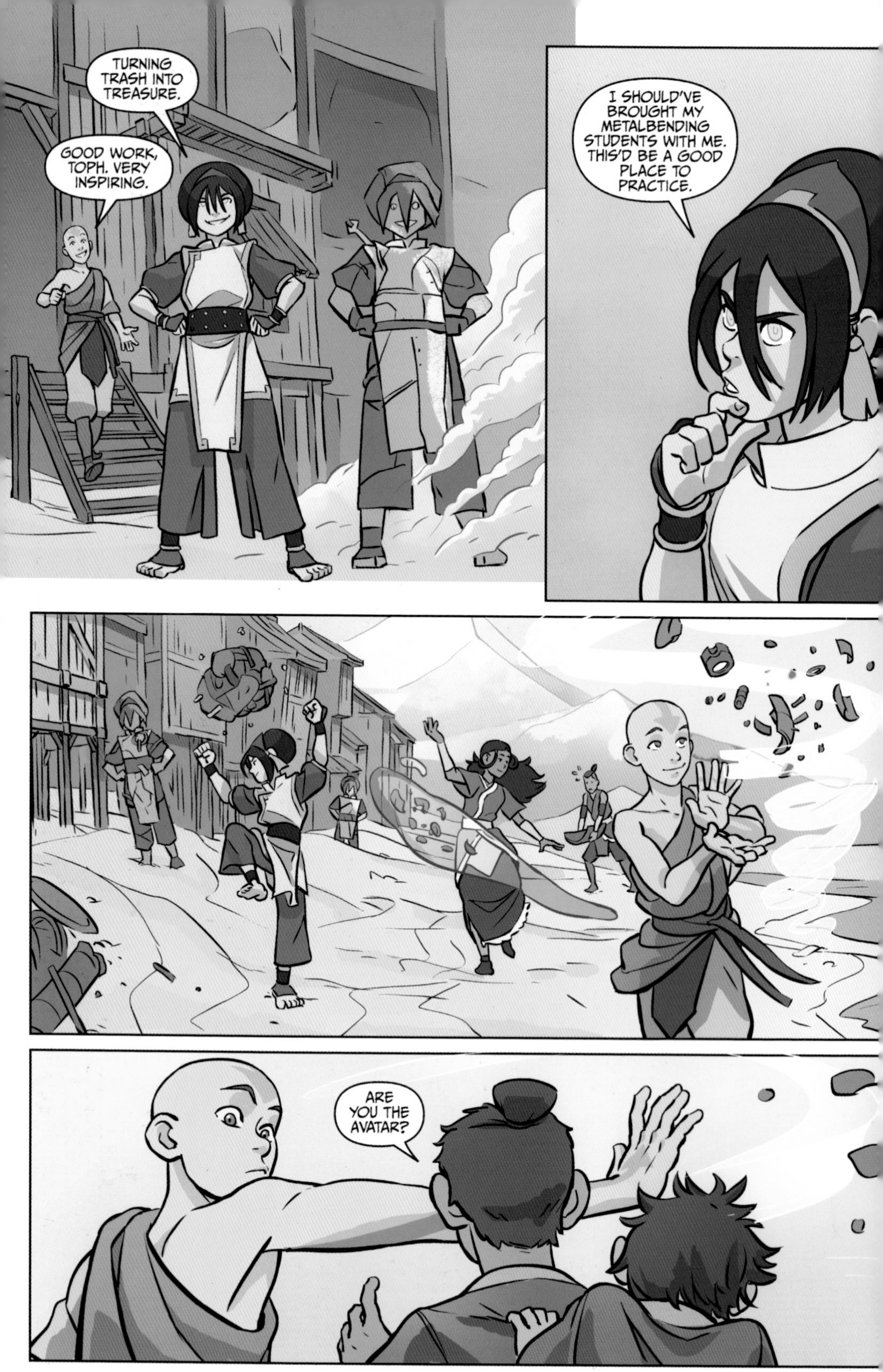
TURNING TRASH INTO TREASURE.
GOOD WORK, TOPH. VERY INSPIRING.
I SHOULD'VE BROUGHT MY METALBENDING STUDENTS WITH ME. THIS'D BE A GOOD PLACE TO PRACTICE.
ARE YOU THE AVATAR?

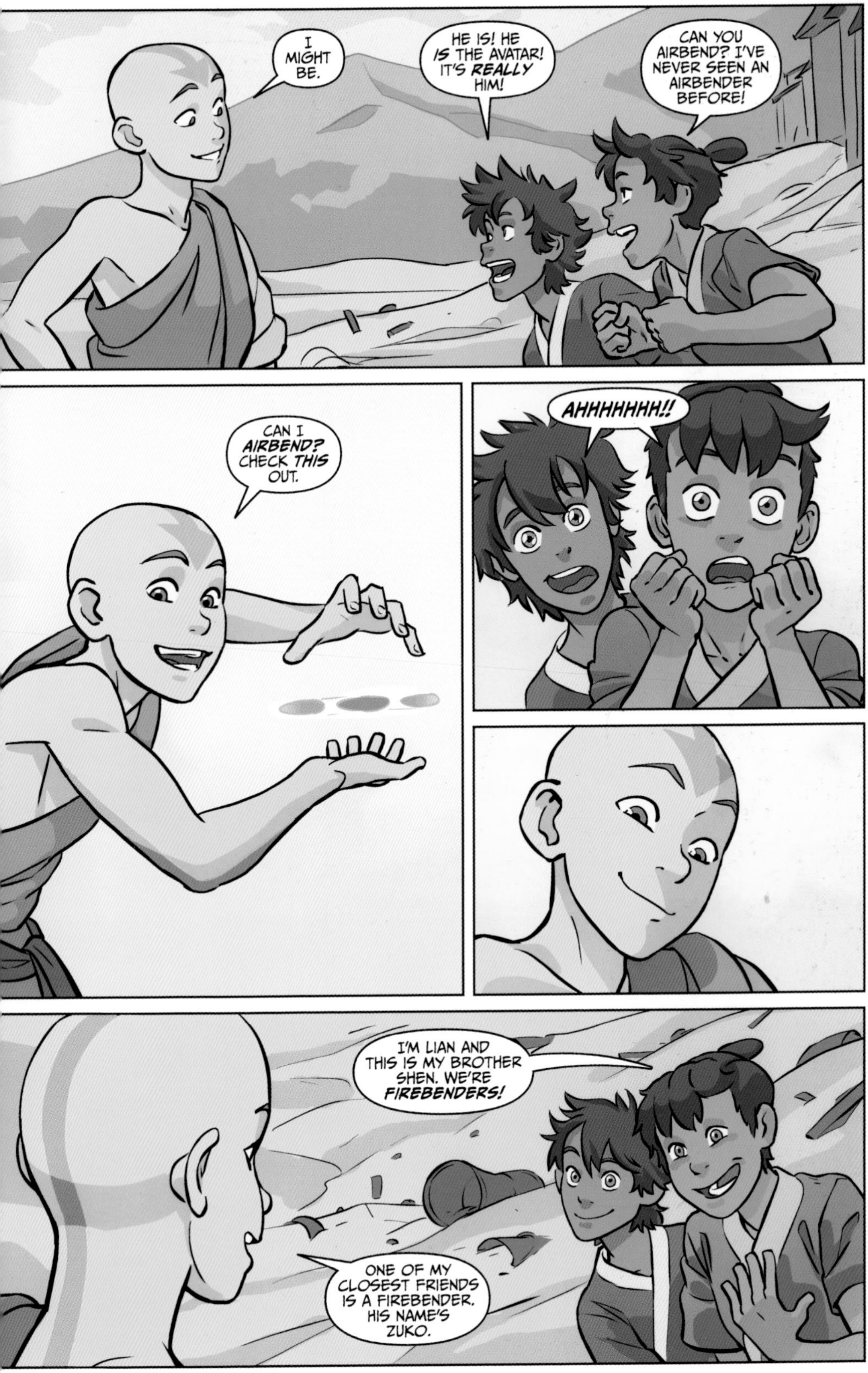
I MIGHT BE.
HE IS! HE *IS* THE AVATAR! IT'S *REALLY* HIM!
CAN YOU AIRBEND? I'VE NEVER SEEN AN AIRBENDER BEFORE!
CAN I *AIRBEND?* CHECK *THIS* OUT.
AHHHHHHH!!
I'M LIAN AND THIS IS MY BROTHER SHEN. WE'RE *FIREBENDERS!*
ONE OF MY CLOSEST FRIENDS IS A FIREBENDER. HIS NAME'S ZUKO.

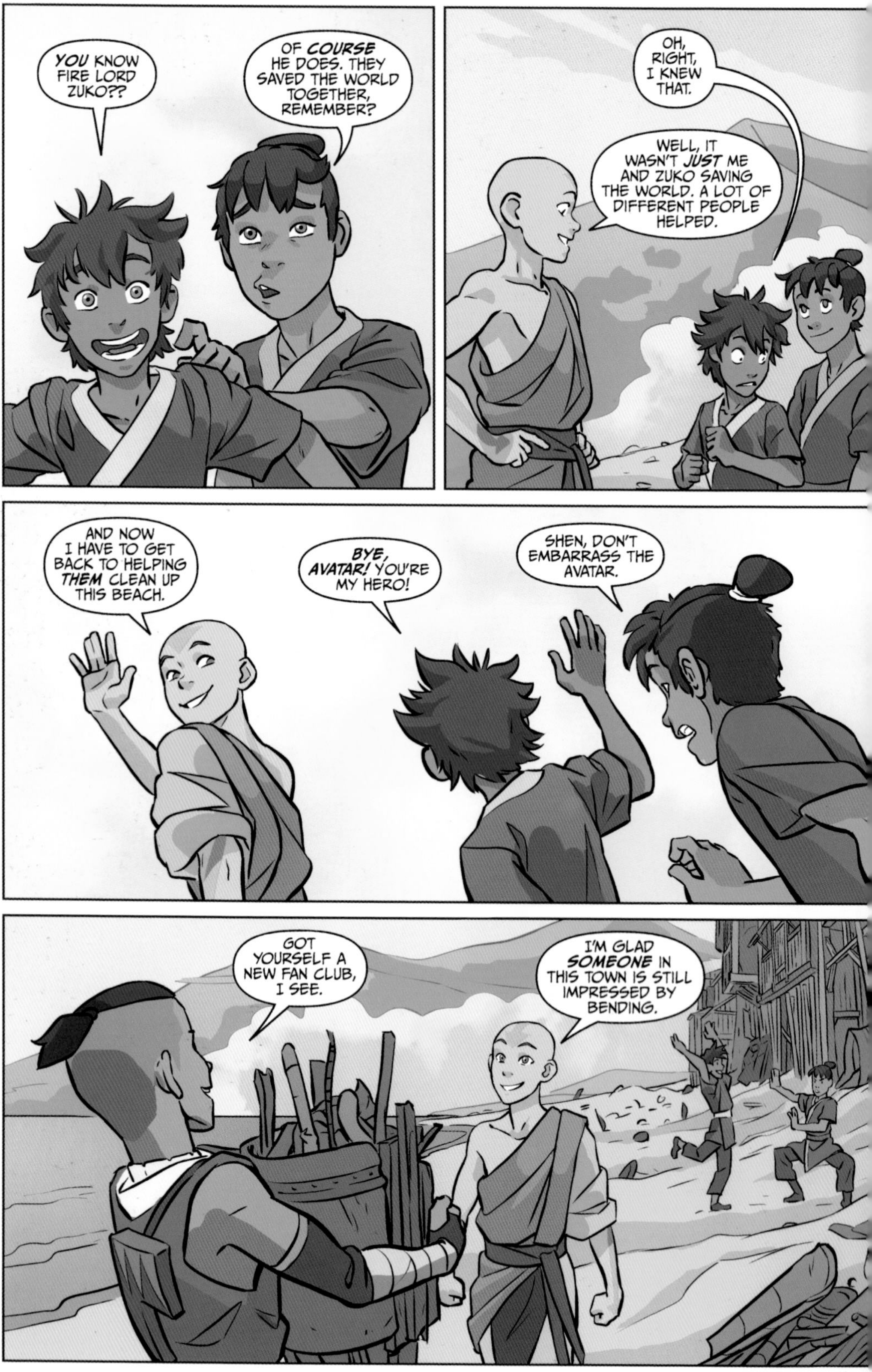
YOU KNOW FIRE LORD ZUKO??
OF COURSE HE DOES. THEY SAVED THE WORLD TOGETHER, REMEMBER?
OH, RIGHT, I KNEW THAT.
WELL, IT WASN'T JUST ME AND ZUKO SAVING THE WORLD. A LOT OF DIFFERENT PEOPLE HELPED.
AND NOW I HAVE TO GET BACK TO HELPING THEM CLEAN UP THIS BEACH.
BYE, AVATAR! YOU'RE MY HERO!
SHEN, DON'T EMBARRASS THE AVATAR.
GOT YOURSELF A NEW FAN CLUB, I SEE.
I'M GLAD SOMEONE IN THIS TOWN IS STILL IMPRESSED BY BENDING.

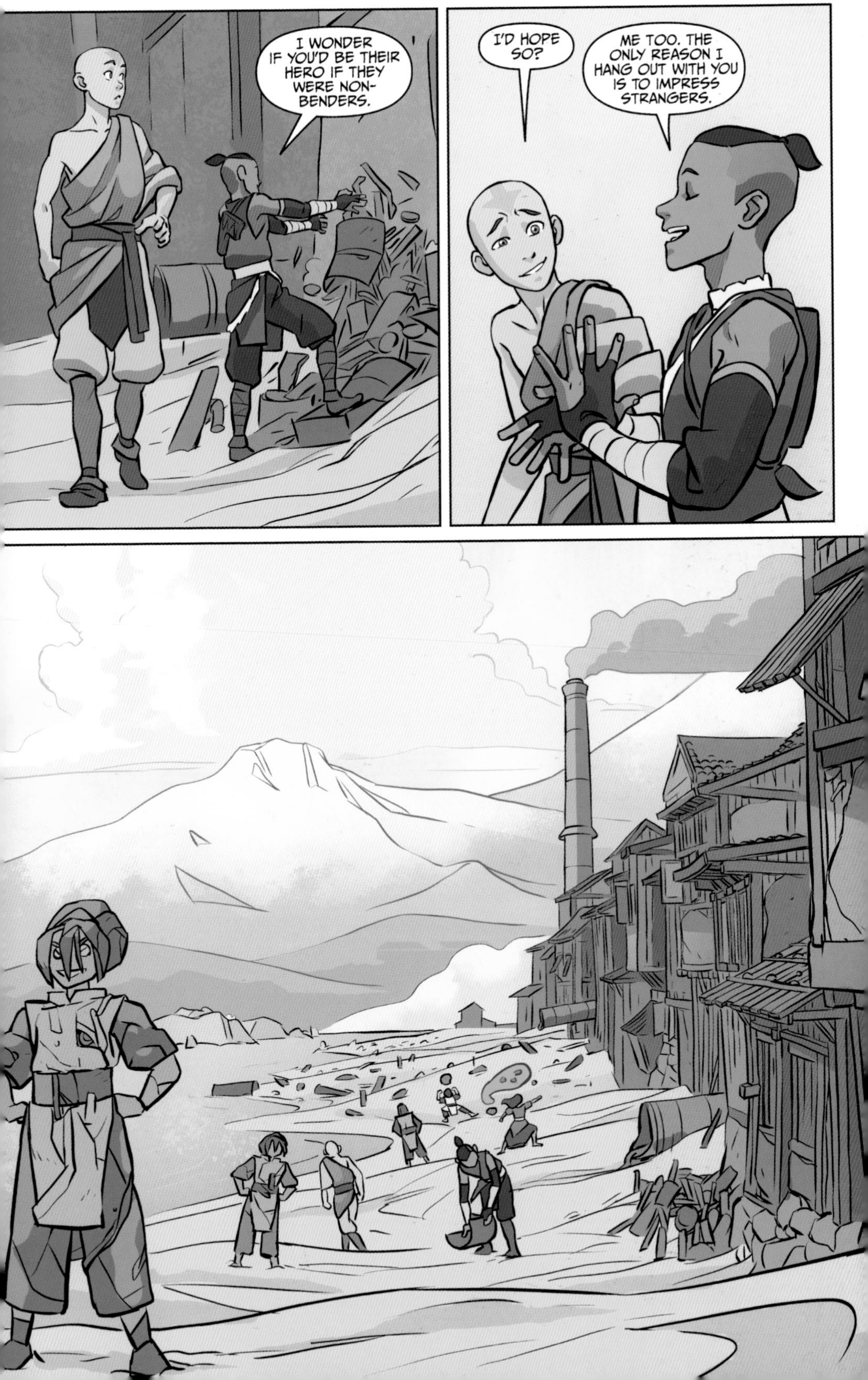
I WONDER IF YOU'D BE THEIR HERO IF THEY WERE NON-BENDERS.
I'D HOPE SO?
ME TOO. THE ONLY REASON I HANG OUT WITH YOU IS TO IMPRESS STRANGERS.

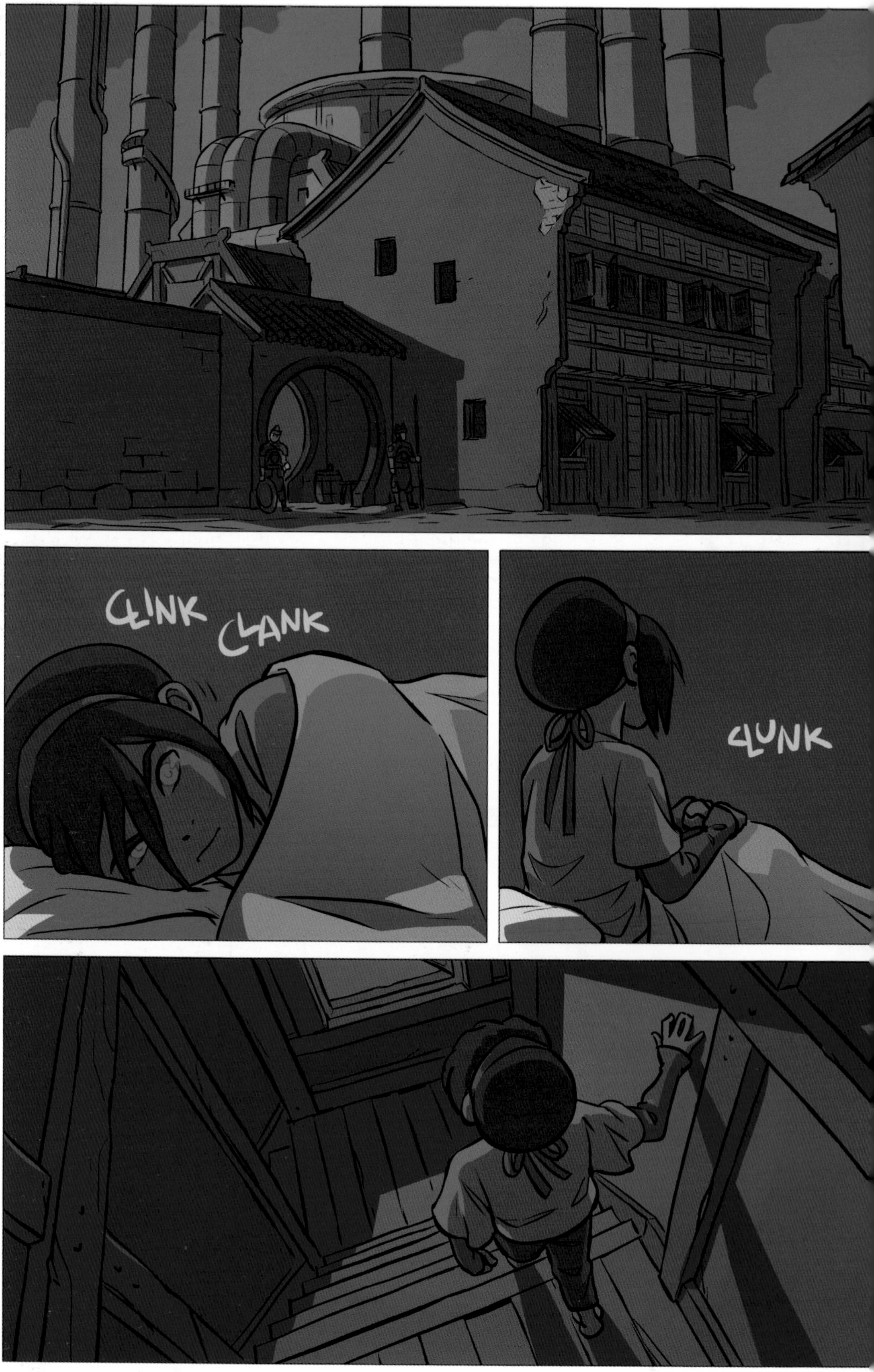
CLINK
CLANK
CLUNK

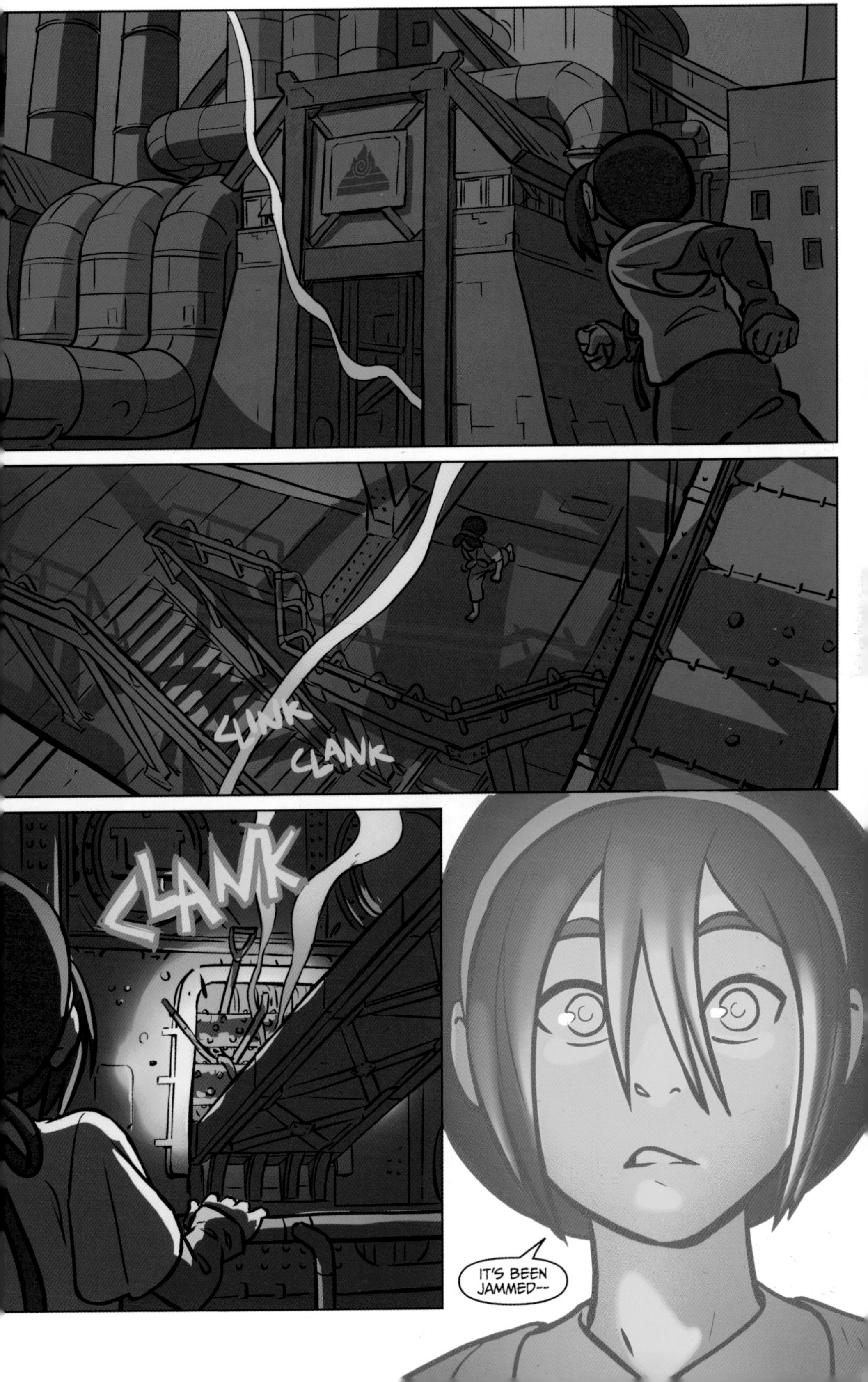
CLINK
CLANK
CLANK
IT'S BEEN JAMMED--

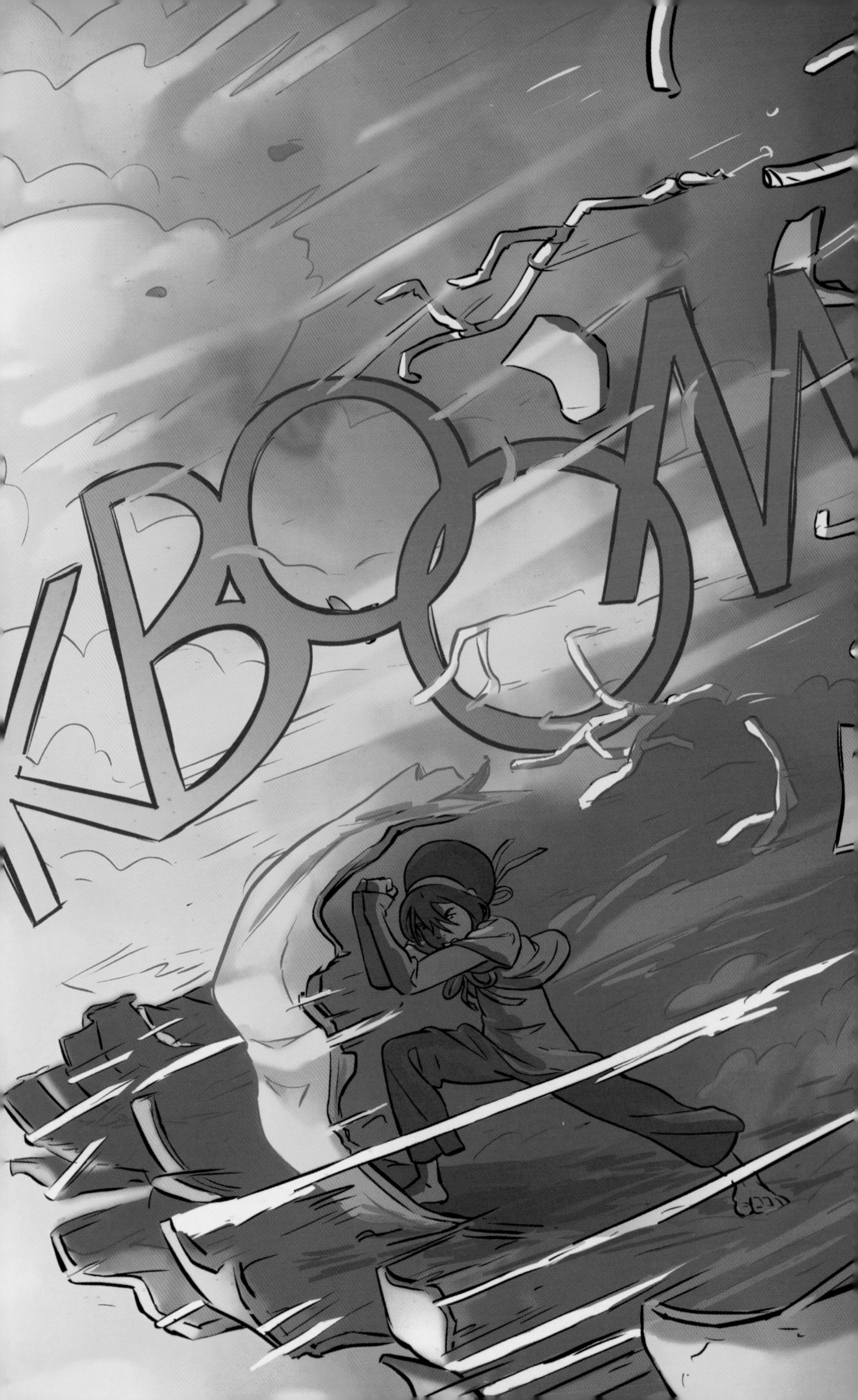
BOOM

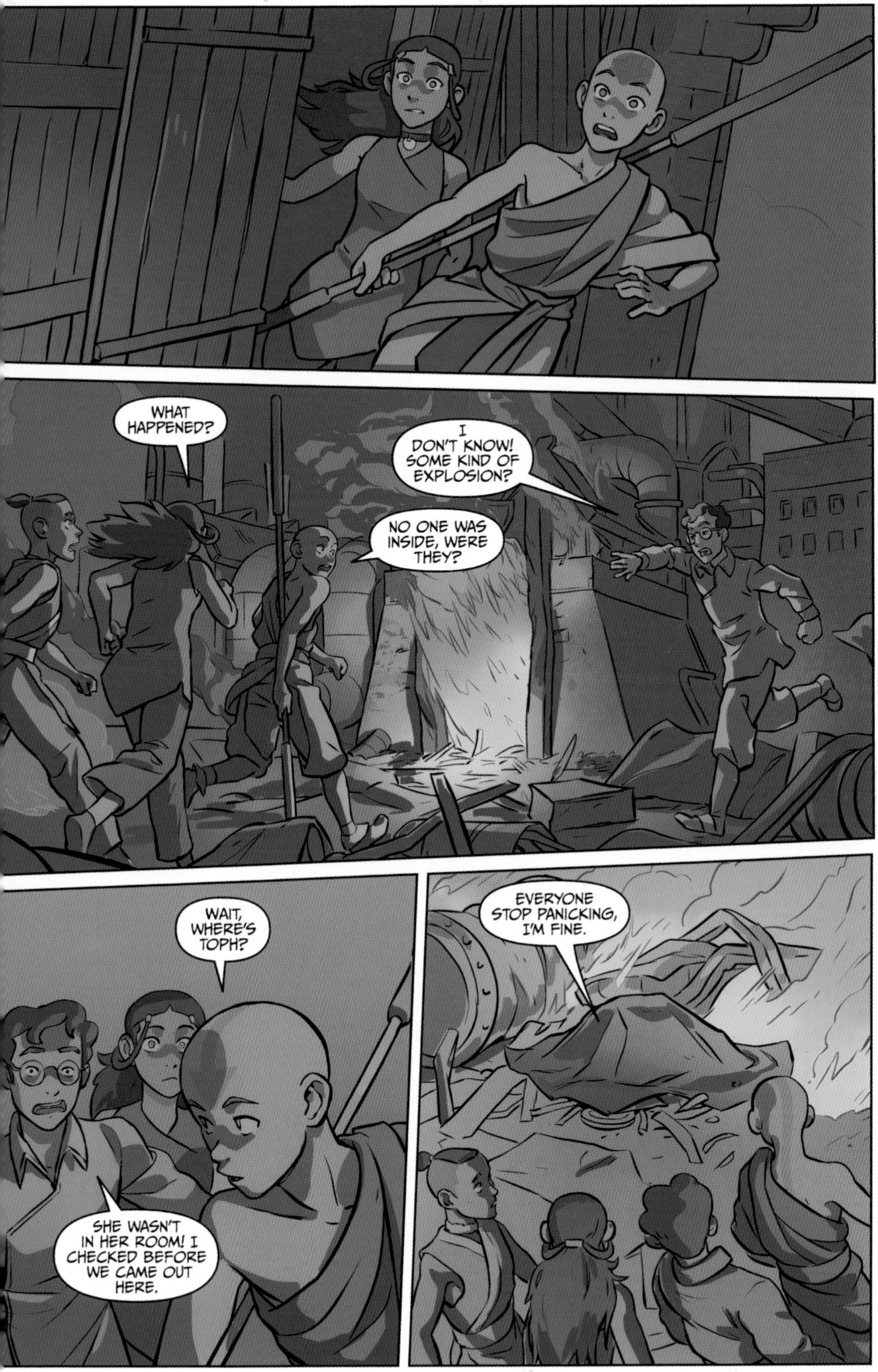
WHAT HAPPENED?
I DON'T KNOW! SOME KIND OF EXPLOSION?
NO ONE WAS INSIDE, WERE THEY?
WAIT, WHERE'S TOPH?
SHE WASN'T IN HER ROOM! I CHECKED BEFORE WE CAME OUT HERE.
EVERYONE STOP PANICKING, I'M FINE.

IT'LL TAKE A LOT MORE THAN AN EXPLODING FACTORY TO TAKE ME OUT.

GLAD YOU'RE OKAY--

DON'T DISTRACT ME, TWINKLE TOES. I NEED TO LISTEN.

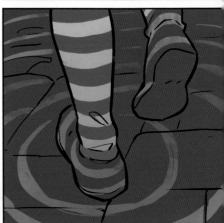

THERE! TWO PEOPLE RUNNING DOWN THAT ALLEY-WAY! PROBABLY THE SAME PEOPLE WHO SABOTAGED THE MACHINE.

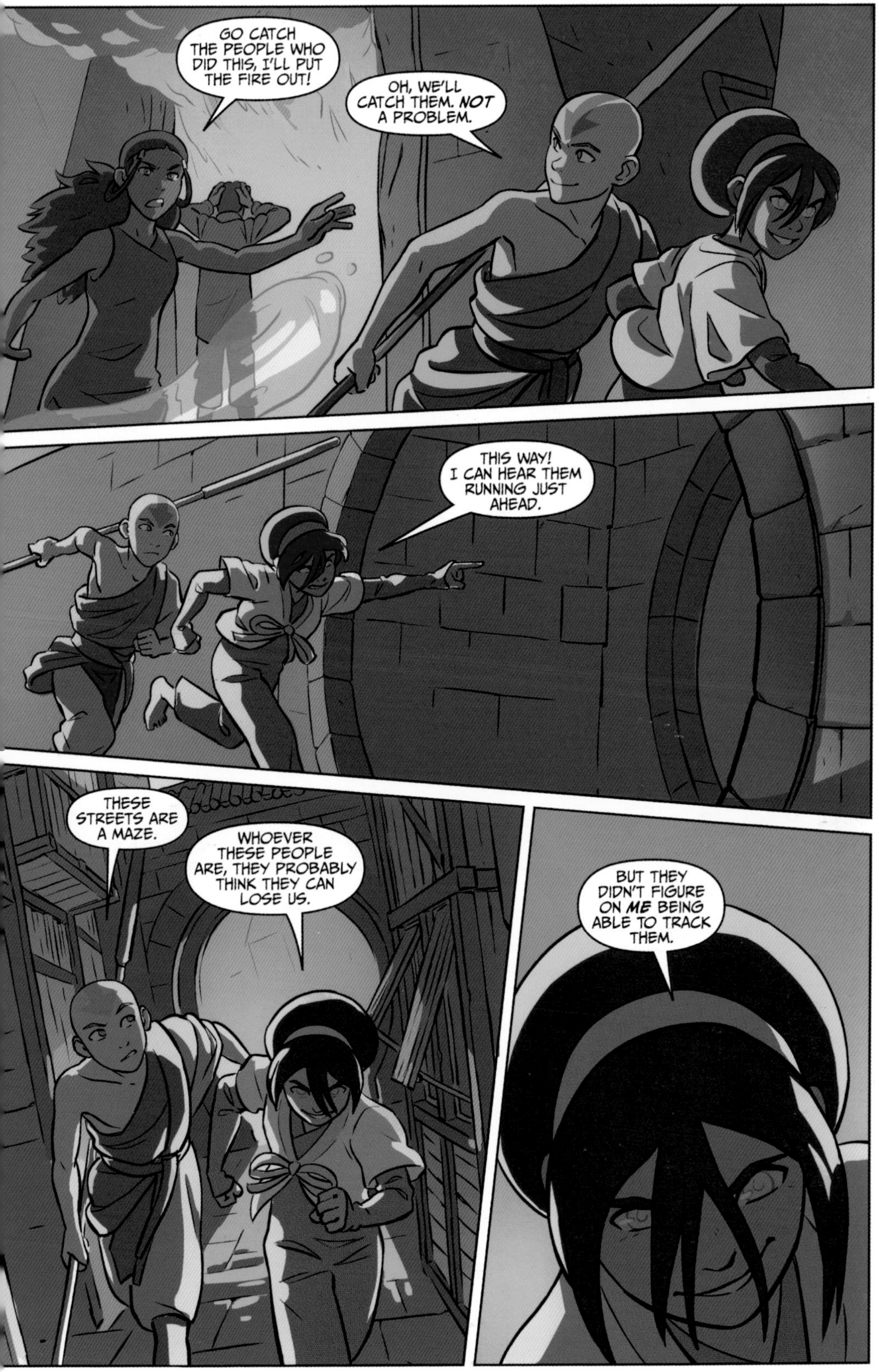
GO CATCH THE PEOPLE WHO DID THIS, I'LL PUT THE FIRE OUT!
OH, WE'LL CATCH THEM. NOT A PROBLEM.
THIS WAY! I CAN HEAR THEM RUNNING JUST AHEAD.
THESE STREETS ARE A MAZE.
WHOEVER THESE PEOPLE ARE, THEY PROBABLY THINK THEY CAN LOSE US.
BUT THEY DIDN'T FIGURE ON ME BEING ABLE TO TRACK THEM.

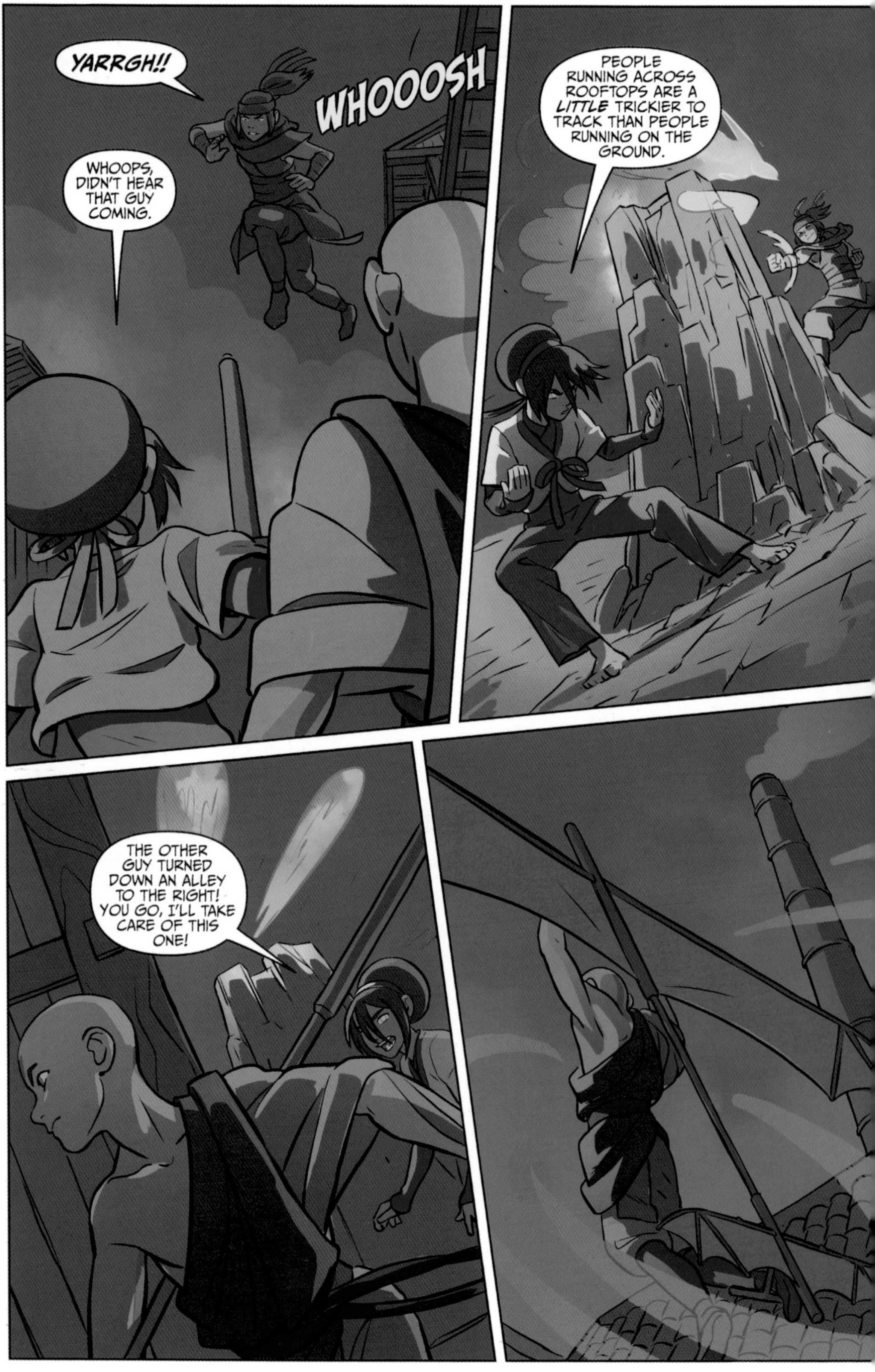
YARRGH!!
WHOOOSH
WHOOPS, DIDN'T HEAR THAT GUY COMING.
PEOPLE RUNNING ACROSS ROOFTOPS ARE A *LITTLE* TRICKIER TO TRACK THAN PEOPLE RUNNING ON THE GROUND.
THE OTHER GUY TURNED DOWN AN ALLEY TO THE RIGHT! YOU GO, I'LL TAKE CARE OF THIS ONE!

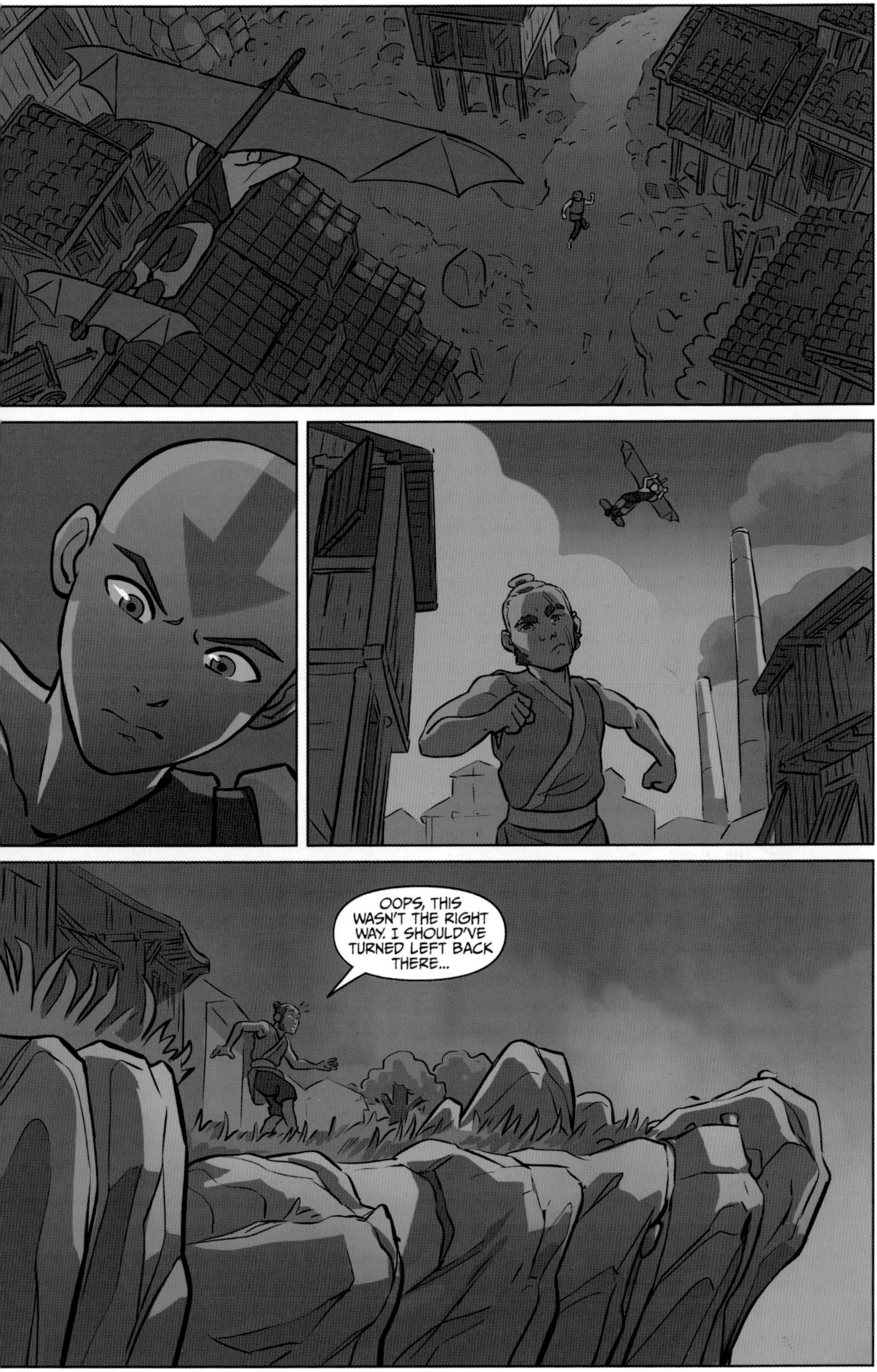
OOPS, THIS WASN'T THE RIGHT WAY. I SHOULD'VE TURNED LEFT BACK THERE...

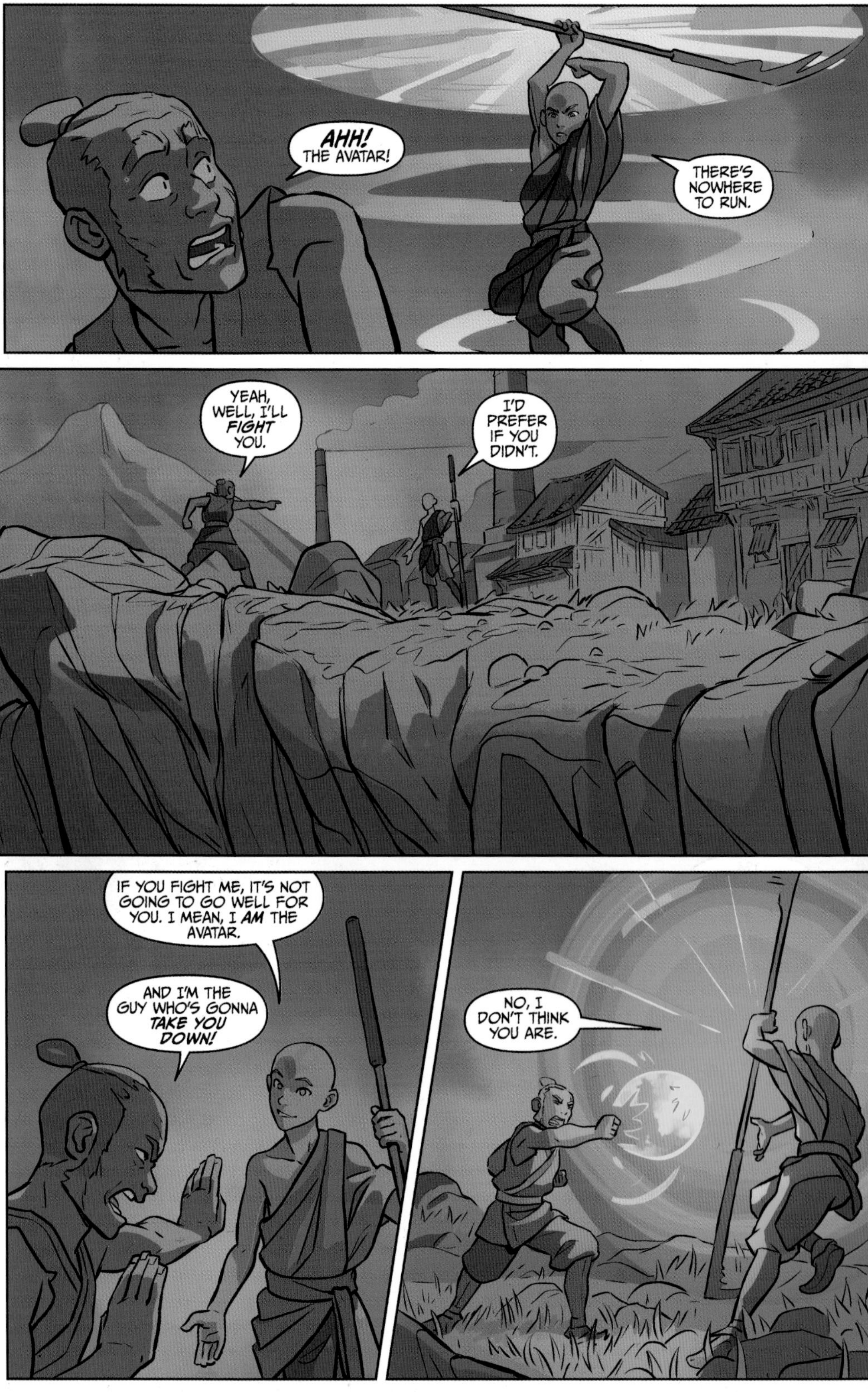
AHH! THE AVATAR!
THERE'S NOWHERE TO RUN.
YEAH, WELL, I'LL FIGHT YOU.
I'D PREFER IF YOU DIDN'T.
IF YOU FIGHT ME, IT'S NOT GOING TO GO WELL FOR YOU. I MEAN, I AM THE AVATAR.
AND I'M THE GUY WHO'S GONNA TAKE YOU DOWN!
NO, I DON'T THINK YOU ARE.

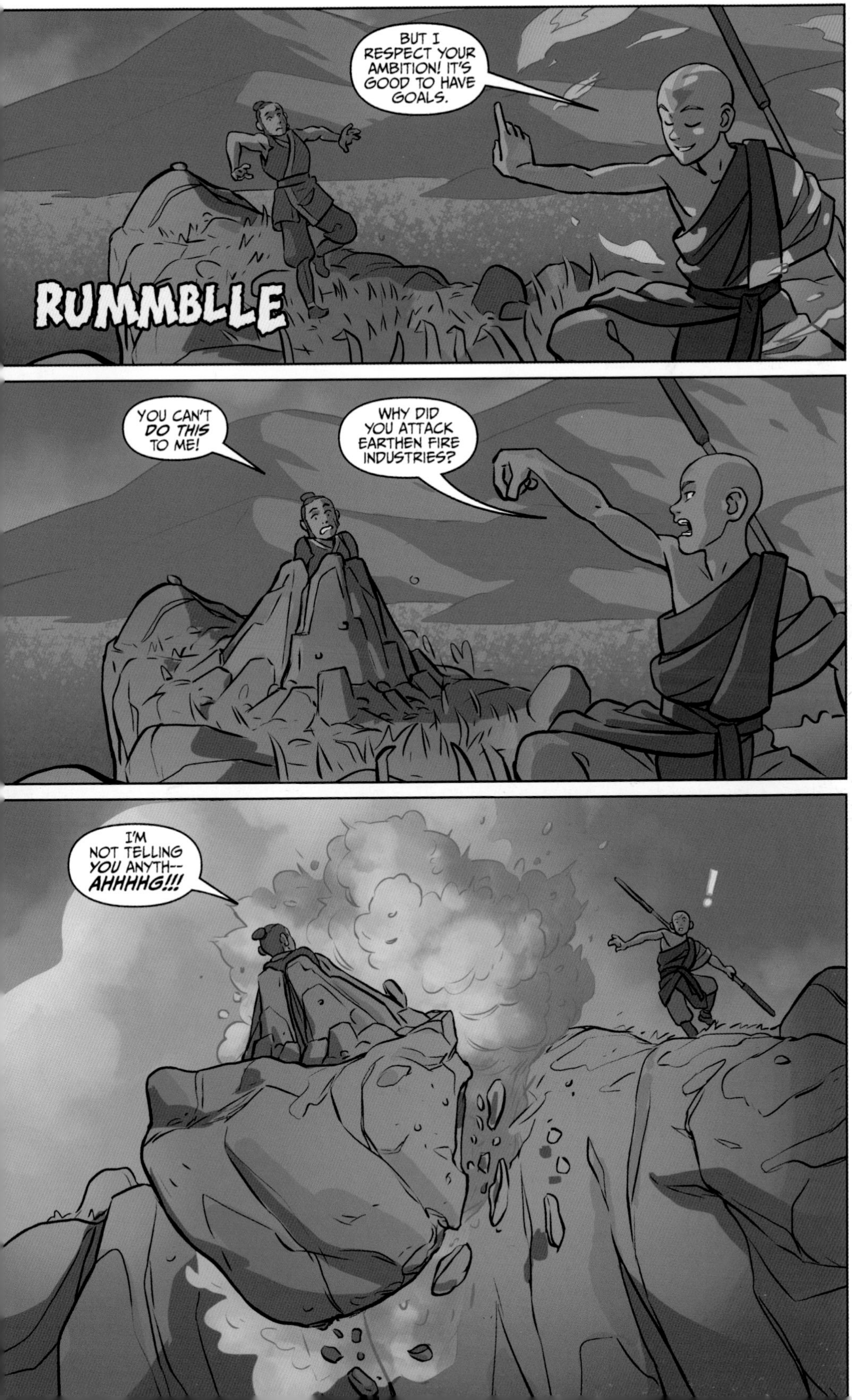
BUT I RESPECT YOUR AMBITION! IT'S GOOD TO HAVE GOALS.
RUMMBLLE
YOU CAN'T DO THIS TO ME!
WHY DID YOU ATTACK EARTHEN FIRE INDUSTRIES?
I'M NOT TELLING YOU ANYTH-- AHHHHG!!!
!

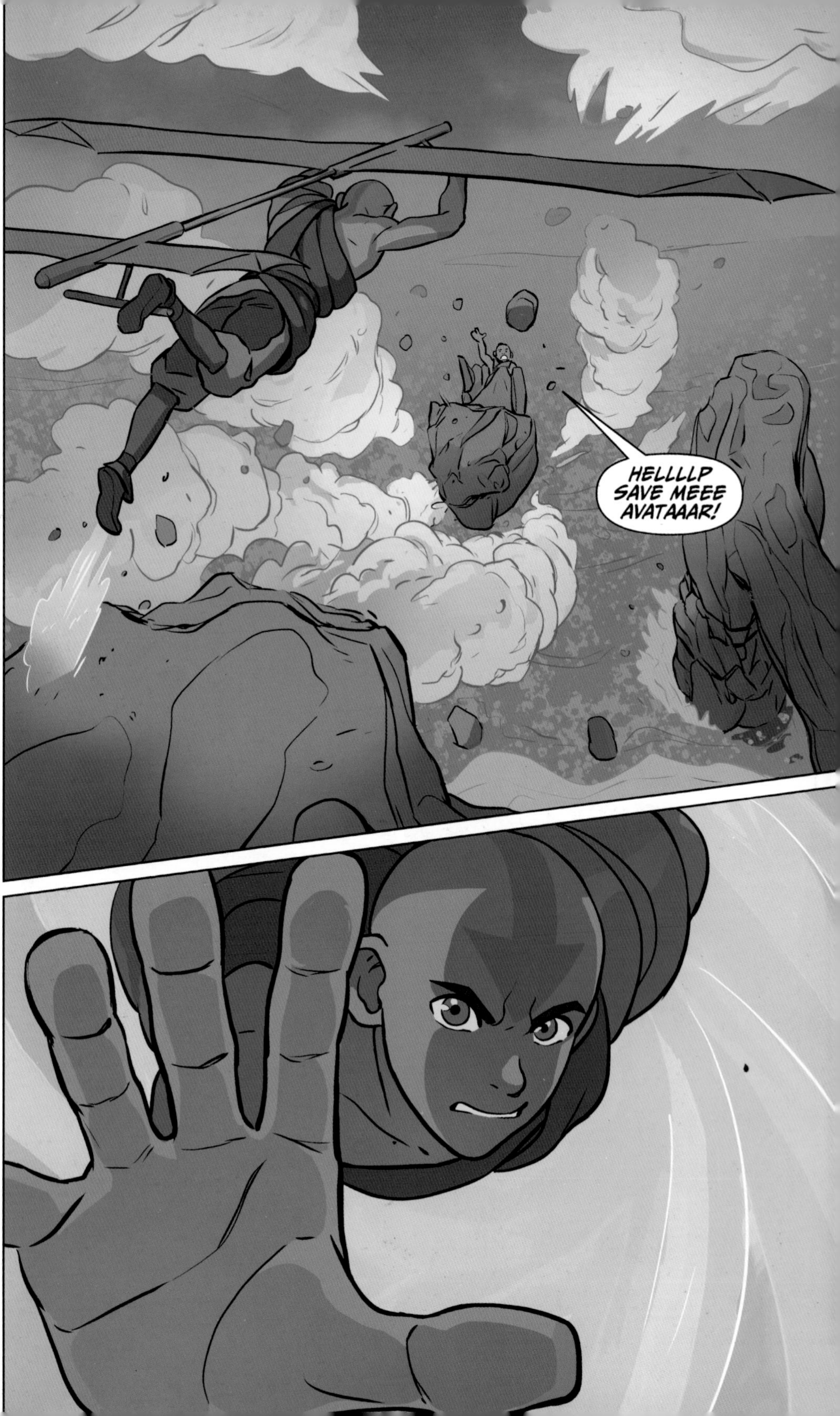
HELLLLP SAVE MEEE AVATAAAR!

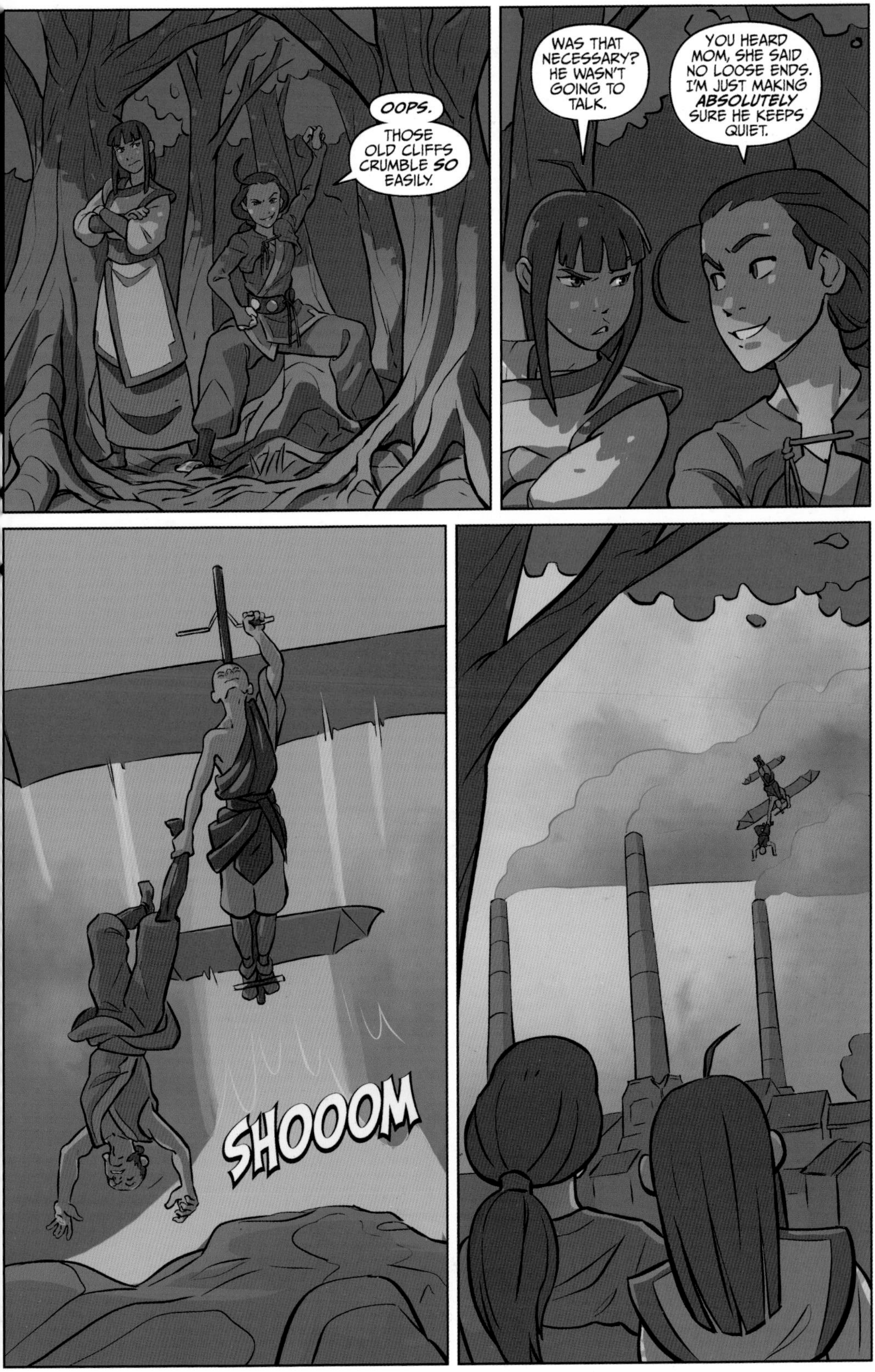
OOPS.
THOSE OLD CLIFFS CRUMBLE SO EASILY.
WAS THAT NECESSARY? HE WASN'T GOING TO TALK.
YOU HEARD MOM, SHE SAID NO LOOSE ENDS. I'M JUST MAKING ABSOLUTELY SURE HE KEEPS QUIET.
SHOOOM

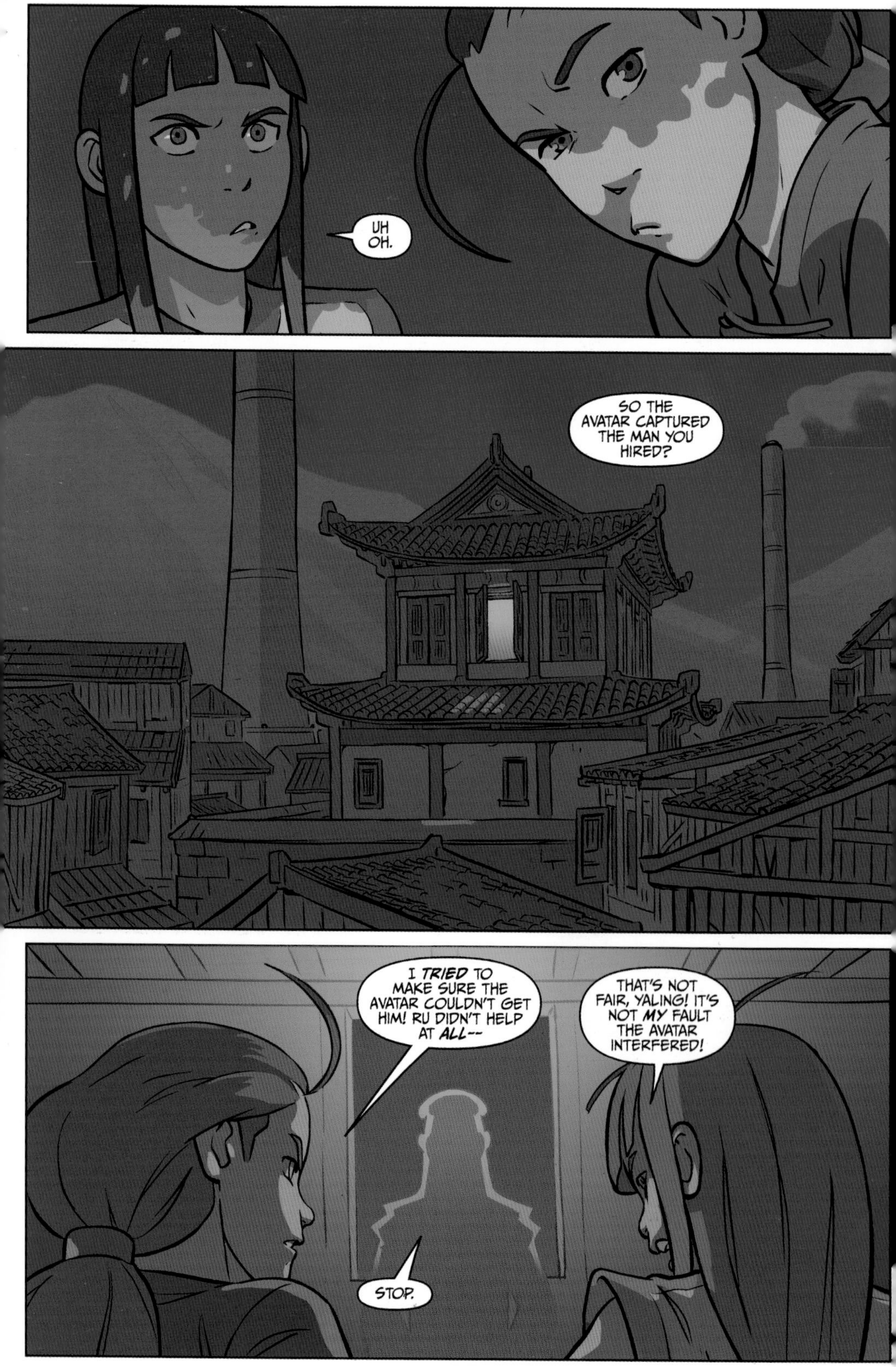
UH OH.
SO THE AVATAR CAPTURED THE MAN YOU HIRED?
I TRIED TO MAKE SURE THE AVATAR COULDN'T GET HIM! RU DIDN'T HELP AT ALL--
THAT'S NOT FAIR, YALING! IT'S NOT MY FAULT THE AVATAR INTERFERED!
STOP.

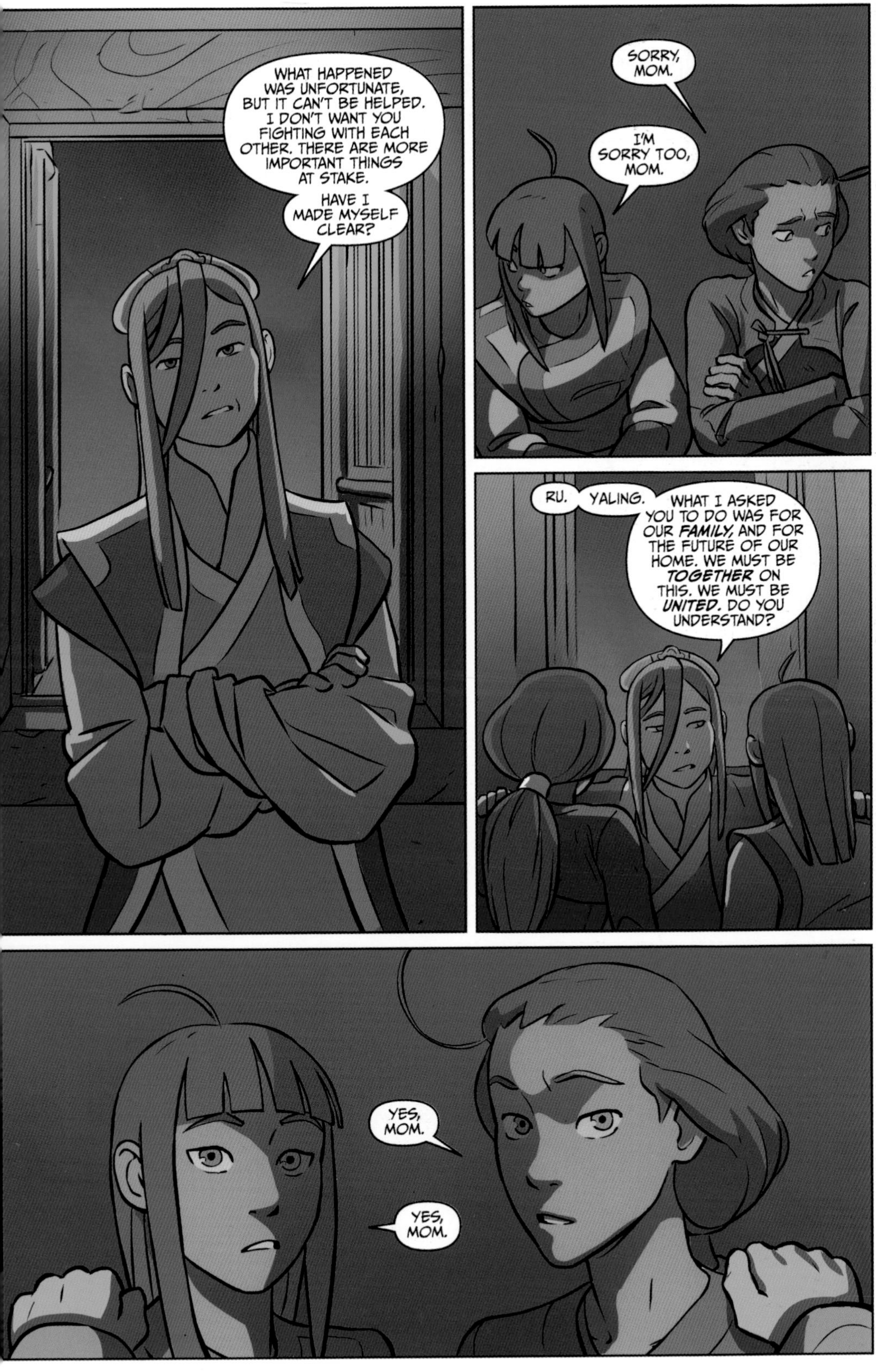
WHAT HAPPENED WAS UNFORTUNATE, BUT IT CAN'T BE HELPED. I DON'T WANT YOU FIGHTING WITH EACH OTHER. THERE ARE MORE IMPORTANT THINGS AT STAKE.
HAVE I MADE MYSELF CLEAR?
SORRY, MOM.
I'M SORRY TOO, MOM.
RU.
YALING.
WHAT I ASKED YOU TO DO WAS FOR OUR **FAMILY,** AND FOR THE FUTURE OF OUR HOME. WE MUST BE **TOGETHER** ON THIS. WE MUST BE **UNITED.** DO YOU UNDERSTAND?
YES, MOM.
YES, MOM.

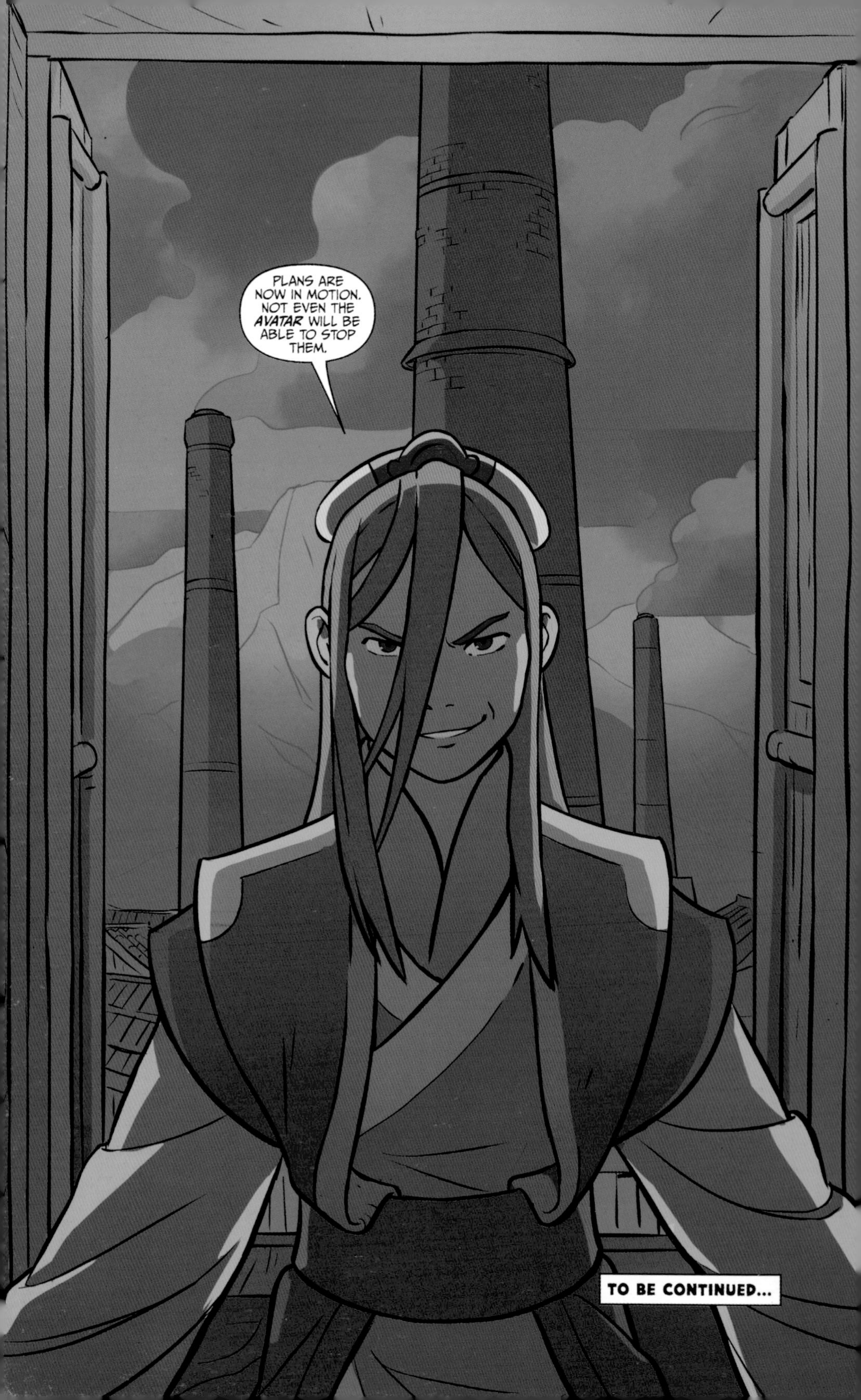
PLANS ARE NOW IN MOTION. NOT EVEN THE AVATAR WILL BE ABLE TO STOP THEM.
TO BE CONTINUED...

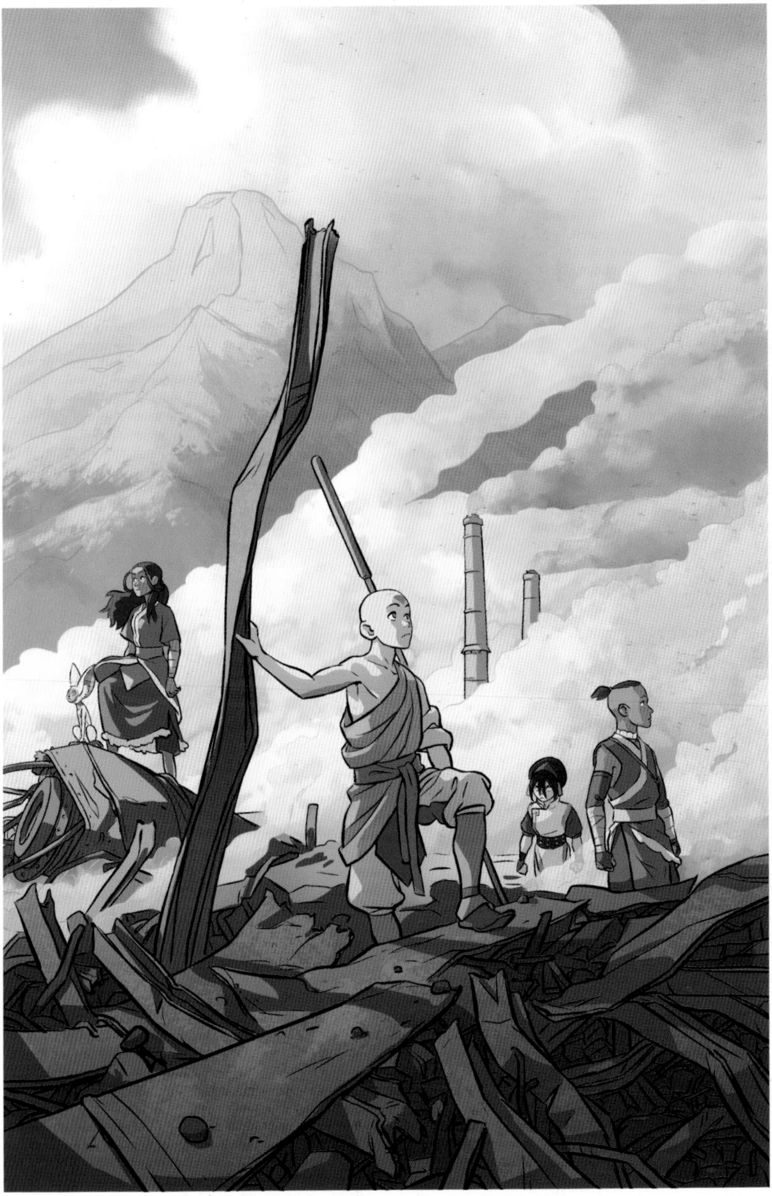

COMING IN MARCH 2019!

Simmering tensions boil over in...

IMBALANCE • PART TWO

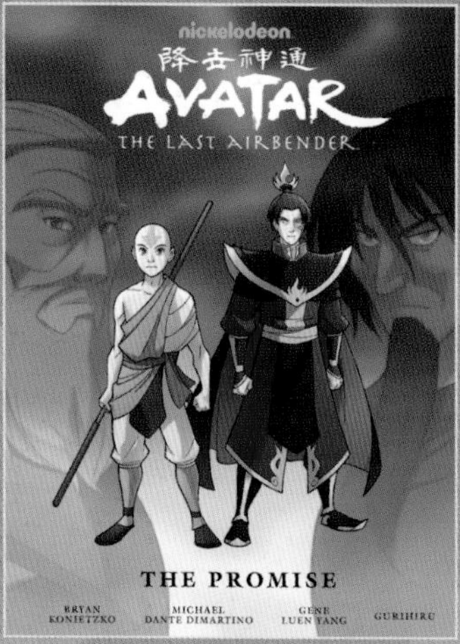
nickelodeon
降去神通
AVATAR
THE LAST AIRBENDER
THE PROMISE
BRYAN KONIETZKO
MICHAEL DANTE DIMARTINO
GENE LUEN YANG
GURIHIRU

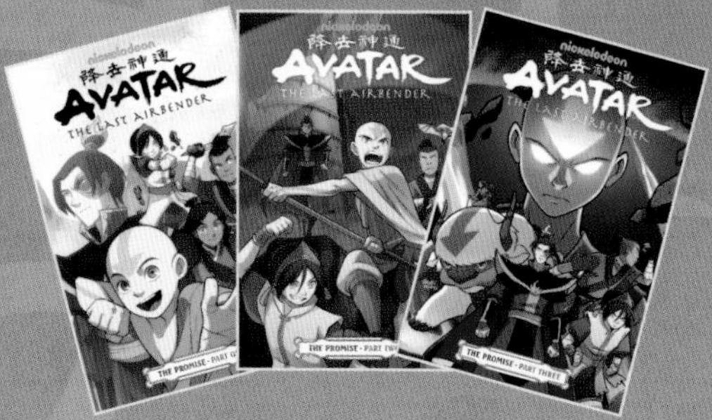
nickelodeon
降去神通
AVATAR
THE LAST AIRBENDER
THE PROMISE · PART TWO
THE PROMISE · PART THREE

Avatar: The Last Airbender—
The Promise Library Edition
978-1-61655-074-5 $39.99

Avatar: The Last Airbender—
The Promise Part 1
978-1-59582-811-8 $10.99

Avatar: The Last Airbender—
The Promise Part 2
978-1-59582-875-0 $10.99

Avatar: The Last Airbender—
The Promise Part 3
978-1-59582-941-2 $10.99

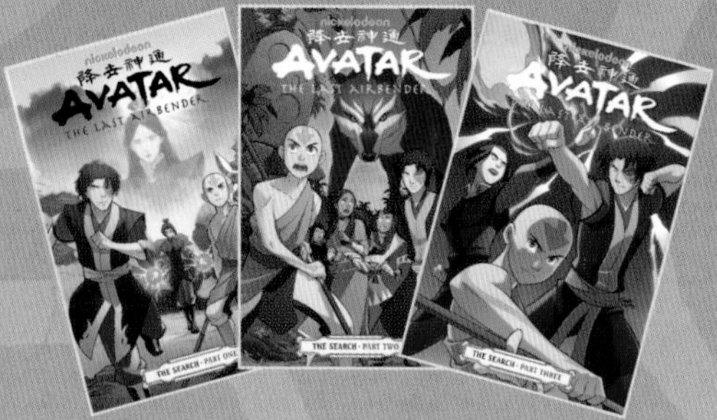
nickelodeon
降去神通
AVATAR
THE LAST AIRBENDER
THE SEARCH · PART ONE
THE SEARCH · PART TWO
THE SEARCH · PART THREE

Avatar: The Last Airbender—
The Search Library Edition
978-1-61655-226-8 $39.99

Avatar: The Last Airbender—
The Search Part 1
978-1-61655-054-7 $10.99

Avatar: The Last Airbender—
The Search Part 2
978-1-61655-190-2 $10.99

Avatar: The Last Airbender—
The Search Part 3
978-1-61655-184-1 $10.99

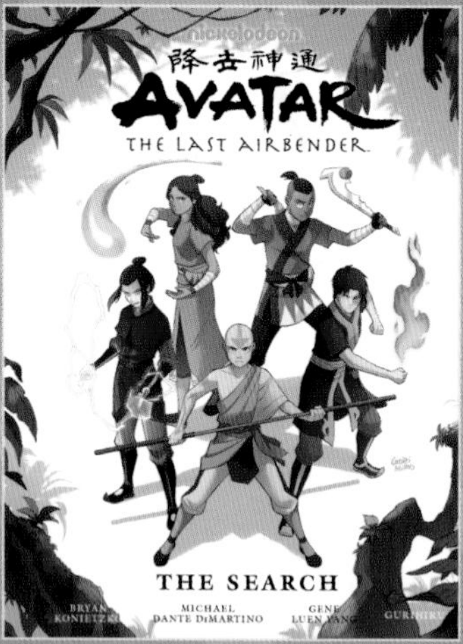
nickelodeon
降去神通
AVATAR
THE LAST AIRBENDER
THE SEARCH
BRYAN KONIETZKO
MICHAEL DANTE DiMARTINO
GENE LUEN YANG
GURIHIRU

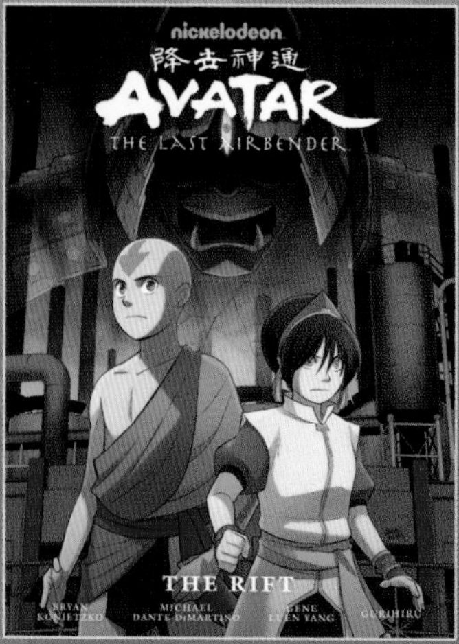
nickelodeon
降去神通
AVATAR
THE LAST AIRBENDER
THE RIFT
BRYAN KONIETZKO
MICHAEL DANTE DiMARTINO
GENE LUEN YANG
GURIHIRU

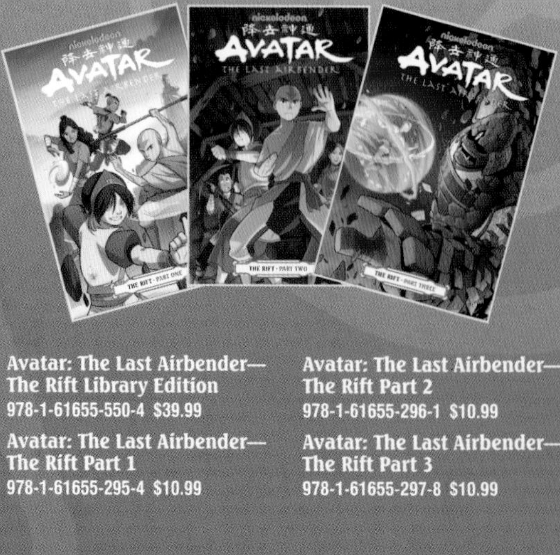
nickelodeon
降去神通
AVATAR
THE LAST AIRBENDER
THE RIFT · PART ONE
THE RIFT · PART TWO
THE RIFT · PART THREE

Avatar: The Last Airbender—
The Rift Library Edition
978-1-61655-550-4 $39.99

Avatar: The Last Airbender—
The Rift Part 1
978-1-61655-295-4 $10.99

Avatar: The Last Airbender—
The Rift Part 2
978-1-61655-296-1 $10.99

Avatar: The Last Airbender—
The Rift Part 3
978-1-61655-297-8 $10.99

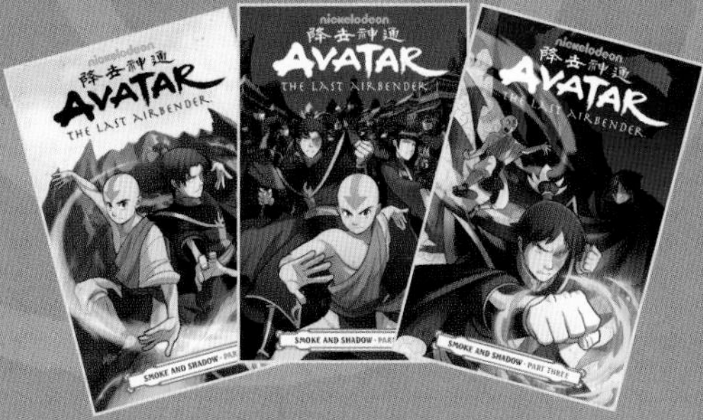

Avatar: The Last Airbender—
Smoke and Shadow Library Edition
978-1-50670-013-7 $39.99

Avatar: The Last Airbender—
Smoke and Shadow Part 1
978-1-61655-761-4 $10.99

Avatar: The Last Airbender—
Smoke and Shadow Part 2
978-1-61655-790-4 $10.99

Avatar: The Last Airbender—
Smoke and Shadow Part 3
978-1-61655-838-3 $10.99

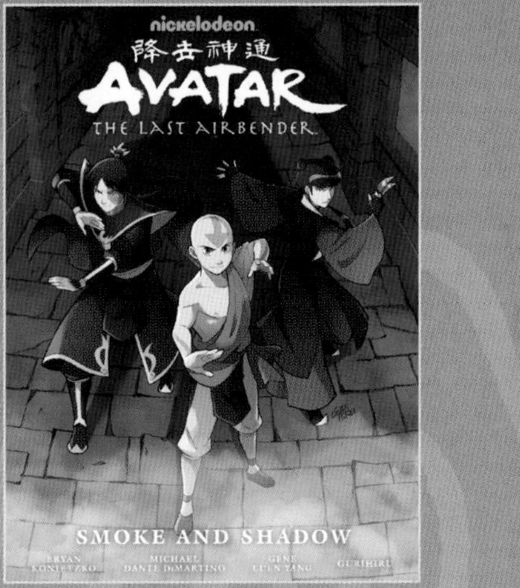
nickelodeon
降世神通
AVATAR
THE LAST AIRBENDER
SMOKE AND SHADOW
BRYAN KONIETZKO
MICHAEL DANTE DiMARTINO
GENE LUEN YANG
GURIHIRU

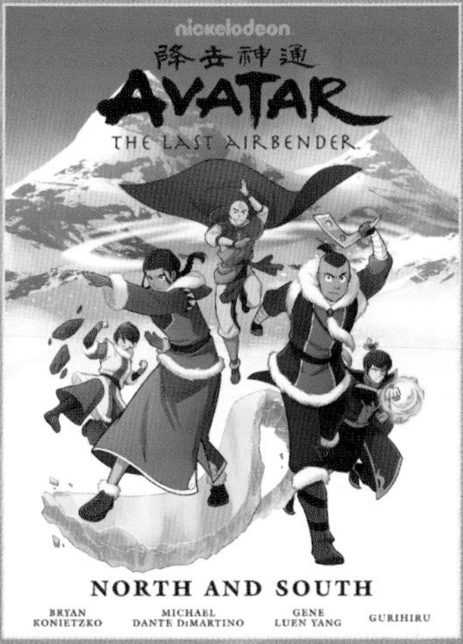
nickelodeon
降世神通
AVATAR
THE LAST AIRBENDER
NORTH AND SOUTH
BRYAN KONIETZKO
MICHAEL DANTE DiMARTINO
GENE LUEN YANG
GURIHIRU

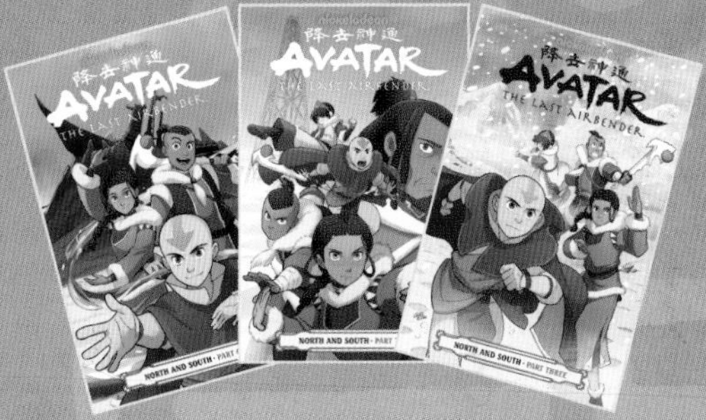

Avatar: The Last Airbender—
North and South Part 1
978-1-50670-022-9 $10.99

Avatar: The Last Airbender—
North and South Part 2
978-1-50670-129-5 $10.99

Avatar: The Last Airbender—
North and South Part 3
978-1-50670-130-1 $10.99

Avatar: The Last Airbender—
North And South Library Edition
978-1-50670-195-0 $39.99

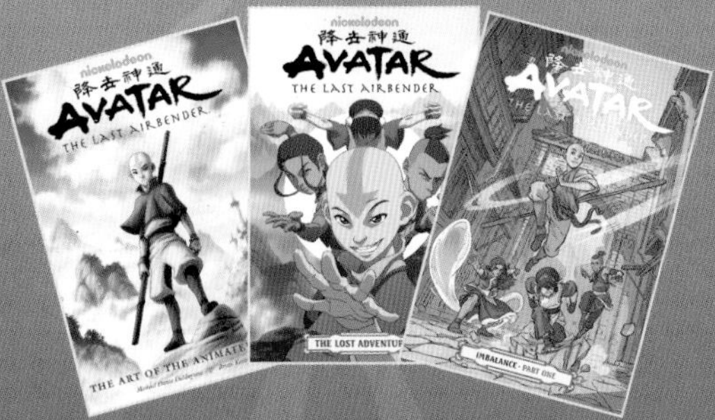

Avatar: The Last Airbender—
The Art of the Animated Series
978-1-59582-504-9 $34.99

Avatar: The Last Airbender—
The Lost Adventures
978-1-59582-748-7 $14.99

Avatar: The Last Airbender—
Imbalance Part 1
978-1-50670-489-0 $10.99

nickelodeon
降世神通
AVATAR
THE LAST AIRBENDER

BE PART OF THE INCREDIBLE JOURNEY!

Check out the best-selling graphic novels by acclaimed writer Gene Luen Yang.

AVAILABLE AT YOUR LOCAL COMICS SHOP OR BOOKSTORE! To find a comics shop in your area, visit comicshoplocator.com. For more information or to order direct visit DarkHorswe.com or call 1-800-862-0052

DARK HORSE BOOKS

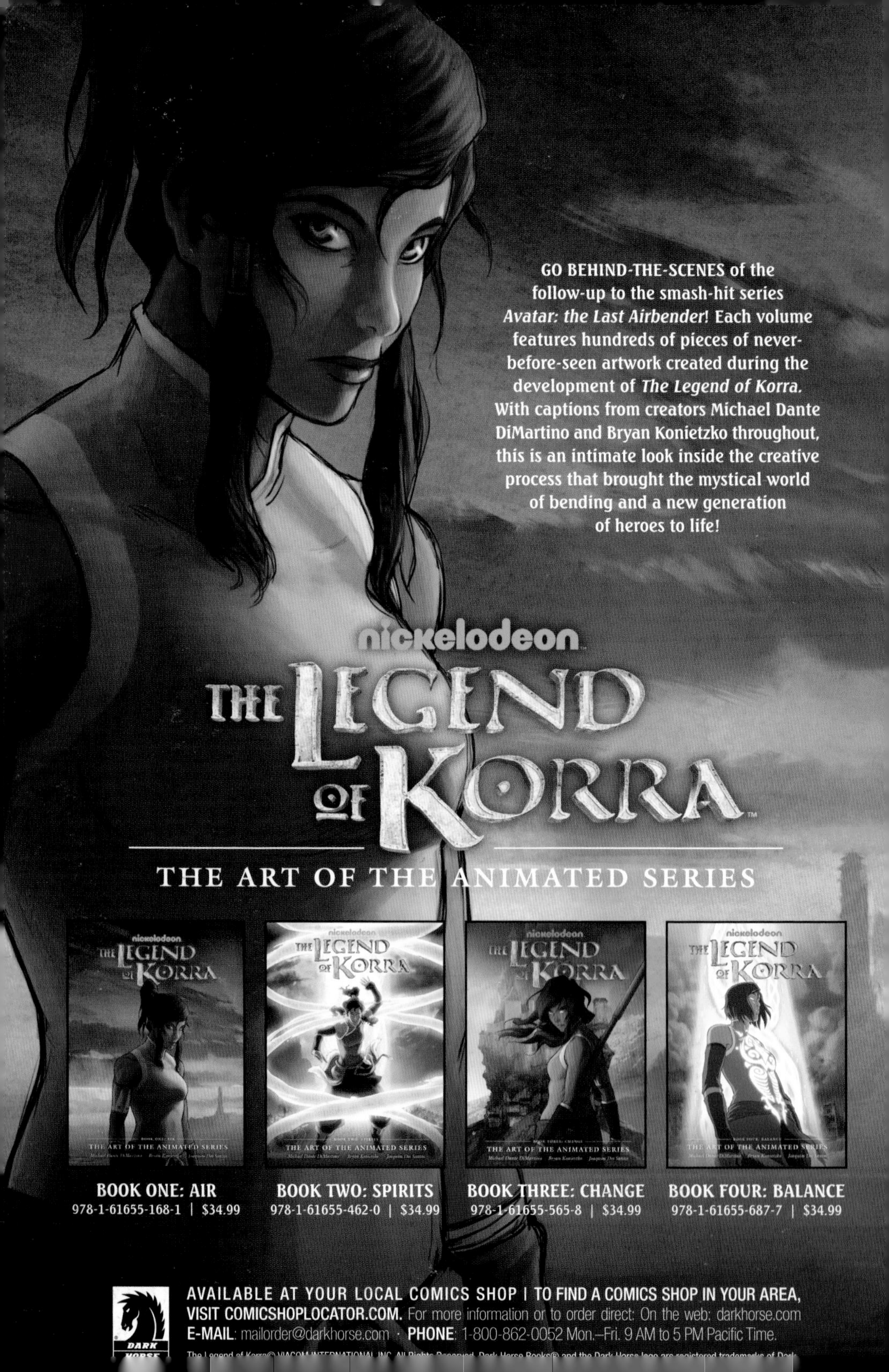
GO BEHIND-THE-SCENES of the follow-up to the smash-hit series Avatar: the Last Airbender! Each volume features hundreds of pieces of never-before-seen artwork created during the development of The Legend of Korra. With captions from creators Michael Dante DiMartino and Bryan Konietzko throughout, this is an intimate look inside the creative process that brought the mystical world of bending and a new generation of heroes to life!
nickelodeon
THE LEGEND OF KORRA™
THE ART OF THE ANIMATED SERIES
BOOK ONE: AIR
978-1-61655-168-1 | $34.99
BOOK TWO: SPIRITS
978-1-61655-462-0 | $34.99
BOOK THREE: CHANGE
978-1-61655-565-8 | $34.99
BOOK FOUR: BALANCE
978-1-61655-687-7 | $34.99
AVAILABLE AT YOUR LOCAL COMICS SHOP | TO FIND A COMICS SHOP IN YOUR AREA, VISIT COMICSHOPLOCATOR.COM. For more information or to order direct: On the web: darkhorse.com
E-MAIL: mailorder@darkhorse.com · PHONE: 1-800-862-0052 Mon.–Fri. 9 AM to 5 PM Pacific Time.